The Expert
Home Baker

Bread Ahead

Hardie Grant

BOOKS

Contents

Introduction

Bread Ahead came to life in 2013, but my journey started long before that. I had always had a love of baking, lucky to grow up in a household where homemade bakes were a regular occurrence. My mum was a keen home baker and dished up some cracking desserts that I still cherish today. So, it was quite a natural step for me to move towards pastry. In 1986, at the age of 15, I began my professional life as a chef in Thackeray's House in Tunbridge Wells. Those foundational years are still to this day what fuels my work and my passion for food. I've had the privilege of working with some of the UK's most innovative and inspired chefs in a number of landmark restaurants. Each person and place has shaped who I am as a baker today.

When the opportunity came up to take on the space at Borough Market, I knew exactly what I wanted to create. Bread Ahead was founded on a few key principles that I'm proud to say we maintain to this day: tradition, quality and seasonality. We favour slow fermentation processes when making our breads and sourdoughs – this is more labour intensive and takes a really strong knowledge of the process, but the end result is more than worth the effort. We also like to stick to traditional recipes, inspired by classic British and European baking. We're not into fads and gimmicks, just good, honest bakes. Of course, seasonality plays a huge role in what we do, too. Surrounded as we are by the abundance of seasonal produce in the market, it's hard not to be inspired by the selection of fresh fruits and veg that change throughout the year. We try to carry all of these principles over to the bakery schools, teaching home bakers to respect the process, to adopt traditional techniques and work with the seasons.

Ultimately, this is exactly what I've tried to convey in this book. These recipes are a collection of personal favourites, tried and tested treats from the bakery school and our customer's top picks from the bakery, which all reflect this very way of thinking.

This past year of pandemic and lockdown was a moment in our lives that I'm sure we will be feeling the effects of for some time to come. However, for many (and certainly for me), it gave us the chance to reflect on what is most important to us. I have been lucky to have been able to use this time to re-connect with home baking. This may sound odd, but it was a moment for me to create dishes in my own kitchen for my own family that might not work in the larger scale of the bakery. I found myself returning to recipes that I hadn't baked or eaten for years. It was a nostalgic journey for me. Sharing these recipes on Instagram showed me how others were connecting over baking at home too, and ultimately it created a whole new dynamic to how we work at Bread Ahead. We created a number of ebooks with some of our classic and newly developed recipes, which proved to be an overwhelming success. I knew that this was the moment to write the second book.

Our bakery schools are a huge part of who we are and what we do at Bread Ahead. We started with one table in the Borough bakery in 2014 and have grown this into five classrooms across London. Our schools give home bakers the chance to develop their confidence and skills. I hope that the guidance in this book will have the same effect and encourage you in your baking journey. The most fundamental piece of advice I offer to home bakers is the importance of patience and practice. Stay committed and you will see great results. I have been baking for over 30 years and I'm still learning something new every day.

Taking the Bread Ahead Bakery School online was another huge step that really opened us up to a global audience. During the 2020 lockdown, we began our Instagram live baking tutorials, connecting with thousands of home bakers across the globe at the same time every day for months. This was one of the most interesting experiences of my life as a baker. I was blown away not only by the sheer enthusiasm for baking, but also by the skill levels so many 'home' bakers had developed. Over the past 18 months, we have built a worldwide community of baking enthusiasts. I have felt humbled to see how one bakery in London could unite people from all over during a moment when we couldn't reach each other physically. Through our online workshops we see how our students have built friendships, share tips and encourage each other through the process. This digital world of baking has been a truly rewarding endeavour.

There are some things that will always remain true at Bread Ahead. We live for tradition. Christmas, Easter, Lammas Day … these moments shape our calendar and, of course, our bakes. Our approach will always remain artisan. There are some areas of the business that will evolve, but as home bakers and professionals there are some elements that will always be done by hand … like the washing up, that will never change.

At the Bread Ahead Bakery School our mission is to build confidence in home bakers. We don't teach you to read recipes, but rather to develop your own baking intuition. We do, however, encourage you to use recipes as a formula and foundation on which to to build. Each chapter in this book offers bakes of differing complexity and requiring varying levels of skill. We recommend starting with the more foundational recipes and working your way up to the more complex bakes as you build on your knowledge and skills. Don't let this stop you from diving straight in, though! If there's a particular recipe that's jumping out at you, then go for it. Passion and enthusiasm will always yield great results.

There are certain key factors to remember as you work your way through this book. Always read the recipes a few times before you start baking – you'll feel more prepared and go into it more relaxed. Look at how long it takes and plan ahead. Weigh out your ingredients and have all the kit to hand before you start. These are your first steps to success. Your equipment and ingredients will also play a role in the end results – the butter you use, the type of flour, the efficiency of your oven – so get to know your kitchen and the ingredients you use. Finally, explore your own creativity. We are here to guide you, so take these recipes, master them and make them your own.

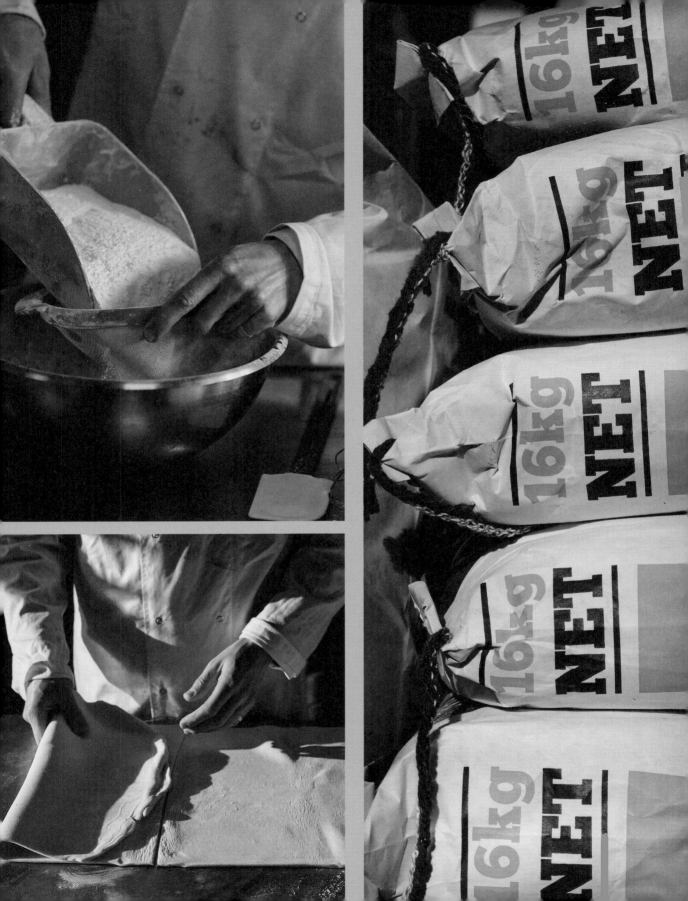

The commitment

From my perspective, baking is quite simply a way of life. I feel incredibly fortunate to have found baking for many reasons. Yes, to a great extent I am somewhat of a 'bakery geek' (the first thing I will do when I travel anywhere is look for a local bakery to see what they are up to – usually this will lead to an interesting conversation with a like-minded soul), but it's important to remember that baking is a craft and, like all crafts, it takes dedication, practice and patience to master. From my experience, I do believe that anyone can learn to bake fabulous bread. It really is about sticking to the key principles and following the basic rules of the game. Once you understand this, you are well on the way.

Preparation

This is really key. Many recipes are in two stages. We often use either a sourdough starter or a 'pre-ferment', which needs to be made or refreshed the day before. This process will activate the yeast cells and develop lovely, natural flavours. It is a process that simply requires time and there is just no shortcut for this.

Weighing ingredients

This is another absolute must. There is no way even the most experienced baker can guess how much water or salt to put in a recipe. All of our recipes are weighed in grams (including liquids) with electronic scales. If you work in a commercial bakery, you will notice that this is a fundamental part of the process the world over. For the best results, always weigh your ingredients.

Where volume measurements are given, use a proper set of measuring spoons. All teaspoon and tablespoon measurements are level unless stated otherwise.

Temperature

Warmth – or lack of it – is one of the most common problems home bakers come up against. Especially when making small doughs (1 kg/2 lb 4 oz, or less), it is critical that the dough temperature is kept at 24ºC (75°F) or slightly above to activate the yeast, otherwise it will not rise, no matter what you do. It is essential that you keep in mind the final temperature of a dough at the mixing stage. It needs to be in the range of 24–27ºC (75–80°F). It is a good idea to use a probe thermometer to test the inside of the dough to check this.

'Room temperature water' can also be very deceptive, so do use a thermometer to keep track. It can vary from 16–24ºC (60–75°F), depending on the room. If in doubt, we suggest going to the warmer side of things to make sure your yeast gets enough warmth to activate. We recommend 24°C (75°F) as a guide for 'room temperature'.

Dough textures

Another common problem for new bakers is mixing the doughs too dry. Don't be afraid of a slightly sticky dough. With a few hours of 'folding', you will be amazed at how quite a sloppy-looking dough can transform into something springy and bouncy. We often demonstrate this in our Italian baking lessons, where we work with 80% hydration doughs, and you will find the technique on page 28. I can remember the first time I saw this method – I found it extraordinary, almost like some form of alchemy.

Time

It is also worth remembering that almost all doughs need time to develop and rest between the various stages. This is another key point that just cannot be rushed or sped up.

Ingredients

Butter

We always use unsalted butter, as this allows us to control the amount of salt in our baking.

When laminating doughs, try to use the best quality butter you can find. French butter has a high fat content and is ideal for laminating. There is something quite unique about the taste of a croissant made with French butter.

Eggs

We use medium eggs, unless otherwise stated. A medium egg in the UK weighs about 50 g (2 oz). We always weigh our eggs, as this will give the most consistent results every time. Broadly speaking a yolk will be around 20 g (¾ oz), and an egg white around 30 g (1¼ oz).

Water

Some bakers like to be very specific about the water they use, but we believe good, honest tap water is the way to go.

Most of our bread recipes will specify room temperature water (about 24ºC/75ºF). This will help to keep your dough warm and aid the fermentation process. Some recipes will call for cold water, or if you live in a very hot climate you might opt for cold water to slow down the fermentation.

Salt

It's important to use unrefined, additive-free sea salt – it has all the minerals needed to really develop your bread. If you're using salt for flavour or texture, for example with a focaccia, use a lovely flaky sea salt, such as Maldon, for a really great finish.

Milk and cream

Full fat is the only way. When it comes to using dairy in your baking, we must insist on whole cream or full fat, for flavour, texture and an overall great eating experience. You don't want to skimp. In some cases, your recipes simply won't have the desired results if you use low-fat products. Doughnut fillings or a crème pâtissière, for example, will be a little lacklustre without the richness of whole milk and cream.

In most cases, you can successfully swap out cow's milk for plant-based alternatives. Almond and coconut milks are, of course, great options for sweet bakes. Soya milk has a good texture for the base of a crème pâtissière or custard, but feel free to experiment.

Flour

The majority of our recipes are based on strong white baker's flour. Occasionally, we use soft (or cake) flour, which has a lower gluten content (you can substitute plain/all-purpose flour if you can't find it). We have worked with Marriage's flours for years now, for several reasons. Firstly, consistency is everything, especially when one is making thousands of loaves of bread. We also try to buy produce as close to home as we can and Marriage's are just 40 miles away and pride themselves on milling the best locally grown wheat. Most bakers do have a close working relationship with their miller, as it is such a fundamental part of the process. In my experience, I find it beneficial to get to know a certain type of flour and stick to it. Flours do have a personality, so the more time you spend with them the better the working relationship will be. I know my flour very well indeed!

Cooking Notes

Useful equipment

Electronic (digital) scales
Measuring spoons
Electric stand mixer or electric hand mixer
Mixing bowls (various sizes)
Wooden spoons
Whisks
Bench or dough scraper
Silicone spatula
Baking sheets
Loaf pans (various sizes)
Cake pans (various sizes)
Silicone baking moulds
Silicone baking mats and pan liners
Dutch oven (cast-iron/ceramic cassserole)
Bannetons or proving baskets
Plastic tubs with lids
Pastry brush
Rolling pin
Cooling racks
Shower caps (optional)
Dish towels
Baking paper
Clingfilm (plastic wrap)
Pastry cutters (various sizes)
Deep-fat fryer or heavy-based saucepan
Water spray
Piping bags
Sieves (fine-mesh strainers)
Jam jars with lids
Oven and sugar thermometers
Sharp knives

Ovens

Every oven is unique, sometimes cooking at slightly different temperatures to the stated settings. This can result in over- or under-cooked bakes. Get to know your oven and whether it bakes hotter or cooler than stated, or has hotspots. We recommend using an oven thermometer to work out the true temperature of your oven. You can then adjust the controls to suit or adjust the temperatures in the recipes slightly. It's also advisable to rotate products within the oven to obtain an even bake.

Recipes were tested in a fan oven. For conventional ovens, increase the temperature given by 20°C, or refer to your oven manufacturer's handbook. There is a conversion chart on page 287. Readers in the US using convection ovens should consult their handbooks to convert °F temperatures accordingly.

Electric stand or hand mixers

These make quick work of mixing and kneading batters and doughs, but don't worry if you don't own one. For creaming or beating mixtures together, use a wooden spoon or a firm spatula, and a wire balloon whisk for whisking. They just take a little longer and require a bit more elbow grease to achieve the same result!

Bench/dough scrapers

These useful tools are worth investing in. A plastic or metal rectangle, usually with one curved and one straight edge, a bench or dough scraper can be used to divide doughs, scrape them off surfaces and help to knead. When kneading bread, rather than dusting more flour over your dough to stop it sticking to the work surface, use a scraper to scrape off the dough that's stuck to the

surface, bringing it back into the ball of dough. They are particularly useful for very wet doughs, such as focaccia.

Sterilising glass jars

Wash jars and lids in a dishwasher or plenty of hot, soapy water. Rinse thoroughly, then place upside-down on a baking sheet lined with baking paper and dry for 10 minutes in an oven preheated to 160°C fan (350°F/ gas 4). Handle with care.

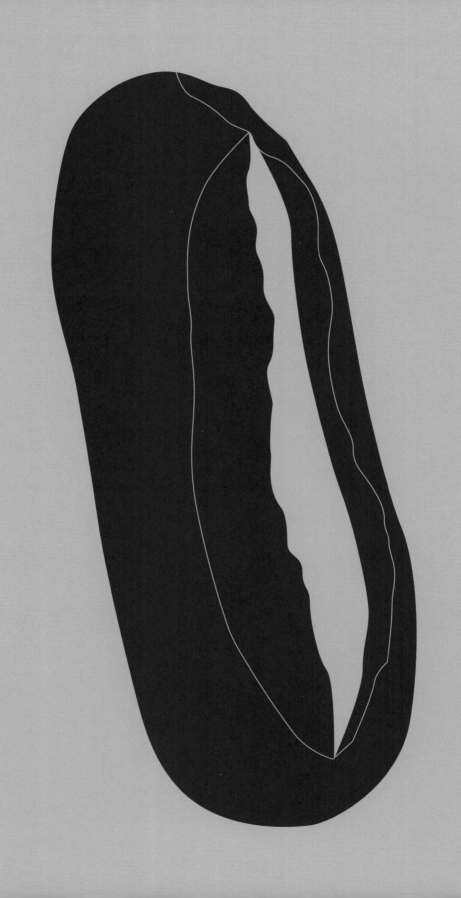

one

Breads

Yeasted Dough

In an ideal world, we would use a sourdough starter for every yeasted product we make. In reality, though, baker's yeast is a good solution to getting a consistent result without the lengthy build process of a sourdough. Commercial baker's yeast also has the consistency and resilience needed for making enriched doughs. It is worth noting that sugar, egg, spices and salt will all slow down yeast activity. For this reason, it is common to see more yeast in enriched doughs, such as brioche, or sweetened doughs.

A few tips to consider with baker's yeast:

- Fermentation time: the longer the dough is allowed to ferment, the less yeast you will need.

- As a general rule, the longer the process, the better the bake will be (up to a point, of course!). A good measure of time is an overnight prove (12 hours), to allow the flavours in the dough to develop. There are two different types of dried yeast – both work perfectly well:

Active dried yeast needs to be added to the water in the recipe (think: active = aqua).

Instant dried yeast needs to be added to the dry ingredients (think: instant = ingredients).

- If trying to work out how much dried yeast should replace fresh yeast, the basic rule is that only half the amount is required, so 10 g fresh yeast = 5 g dried yeast.

Kneading

There's no right or wrong way to knead bread. We teach several kneading methods in our bakery schools. The one thing I will always remind both new and experienced bakers of is the importance of practice. Nothing can replace the knowledge you gain from the experience of just doing it. Try these different methods, but – believe me – this will become second nature in time.

Traditional kneading

The traditional method, with which most people are familiar, involves pushing the dough across the work surface, using the heel of the palm of your hand to really stretch the dough out and thus stretching and developing the strands of gluten. After you have stretched it out, grab the top of the dough and fold it over itself to bring it back to the original starting place (using your hand or a dough scraper if it is very sticky). Repeat until your dough has developed. This is a great place to start as a beginner and in the early stages of developing a loaf of bread.

Slap and fold

We like to use the slap and fold method, too. This is a great way to incorporate a lot of air into the dough. It works really well with relatively high-hydration doughs (as these can be a little too sloppy to stretch on the work surface).

Start by gripping the top of the dough and lifting it off the work surface to about level with your shoulders [see photo 1, opposite].

Next, 'slap' it back down on the work surface, folding the top of the dough over itself [photos 2, 3 and 4].

Continue this motion until you can feel the dough become elastic and smooth. You can usually tell when you've kneaded the dough enough as the surface becomes smooth, with good tension, and it stops 'tearing'.

Folding

You'll notice we use a lot of folding techniques throughout the bread chapter. This is absolutely the best way to develop the gluten in high-hydration loaves (such as focaccia, ciabatta or sourdoughs).

A complete set of folds is completed as follows:

Pinch the right-hand side of the dough between your fingers and pull the dough upwards, folding it over itself to the left-hand side. Repeat this from left to right, from front to back, then finally from the back to the front. Leave the dough to rest between folds, as this is critical to the gluten development.

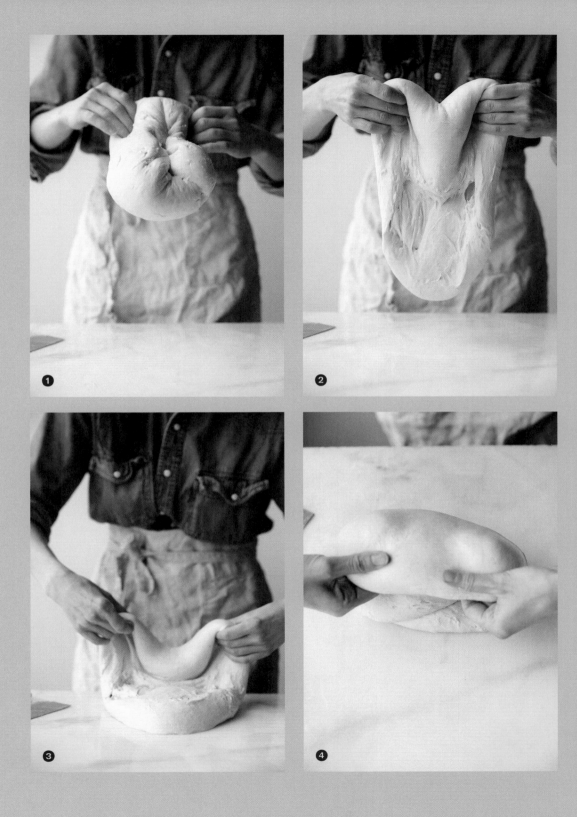

Stitching

We refer to the stitching method in our Rustic Country Loaf on page 50. This technique is commonly seen in sourdough baking and is a very simple way to shape your loaf, build tension on the surface and seal the seam of your loaf. It is very much like swaddling a baby.

Place your dough out in front of you (in a rough rectangle shape). Beginning at the top, grab either side of the dough and pinch the sides into the middle, 'stitching' them together [see photo above]. Continue all the way down the loaf until you have sealed the dough together.

White Sandwich Tin Loaf

The white tin loaf really is an essential part of making a good traditional sandwich and the key to a classic breakfast spread – served with butter and marmalade, it makes the most delicious toast. The Bread Ahead white tin uses a far more traditional approach than its modern supermarket counterpart. Most importantly, we use a long, slow fermentation to develop the flavour.

For the pre-ferment

2 g (⅓ teaspoon) fresh yeast or
  1 g (⅓ teaspoon) dried active yeast
50 g (3 tablespoons) warm water
80 g (3 oz/½ cup) strong white
  (bread) flour
2 g (⅓ teaspoon) fine sea salt

For the loaf

370 g (13 oz/2⅔ cups) strong white
  (bread) flour
6 g (1 teaspoon) fine sea salt
4 g (¾ teaspoon) fresh yeast or
  2 g (¾ teaspoon) dried active yeast
230 g (scant 1 cup) cold water
vegetable oil, for greasing (optional)
semolina or extra flour, for
  dusting (optional)

Day 1

To make the pre-ferment, add the fresh yeast and warm water to a mixing bowl and mix until dissolved. If using dried yeast, check the packet instructions – you will either mix the yeast through the flour, then add the water, or you may need to hydrate the dried yeast in the water first.

Add the flour and salt to the bowl and mix until it has come together into a rough dough. Cover and leave at room temperature for 2 hours, then refrigerate for 12–24 hours.

Day 2

Place the flour and salt in a bowl and combine.

In a separate bowl, add the pre-ferment and yeast to the measured cold water and mix.

Make a well in the flour mixture and pour in the liquid. Gently bring the dough together. Once the dough starts coming together, transfer it to the work surface. Don't add any flour.

Push the dough into the table with the heel of your hand and knead for about 8 minutes. The dough will become elasticated and have a velvety feel. Form the dough into a round and place it back in the bowl. Cover and leave for 1–2 hours at room temperature, then refrigerate for 12–24 hours.

Continued next page →

3 days
Makes 1 large loaf

Day 1
Preparation – 5 minutes
Resting – 2 hours
Chilling – 12–24 hours

Day 2
Preparation – 15 minutes
Proving – 1–2 hours
Chilling – 12–24 hours

Continued →

Day 3

Release the dough from the bowl – this will gently knock it back, releasing some of the gas and encouraging the yeast to start working a bit faster. Shape it into a loose round shape, then cover again and leave to rest for at least 10 minutes.

Dust a proving basket heavily with flour or lightly oil a 900-g (2-lb) loaf tin (pan).

Shape your dough as desired and place it into the proving basket/tin. Cover and leave to prove at room temperature for 1–2 hours. You can tell when your bread is ready by gently pushing your finger into the dough. If it springs back nicely it's ready, but if it leaves an indent it isn't.

Preheat the oven to 230°C fan (475°F/gas 9) or as hot as your oven will go.

If you proved your loaf in a basket, place a baking stone (or overturned baking sheet) into the oven to heat up. Dust another flat baking sheet with semolina or flour and upturn the proving basket in the middle of the sheet to release the dough. Use a razor or a sharp serrated knife to score the dough.

If you proved your bread in a tin, you can score it down the middle or just leave it as is.

Slide the dough from the baking sheet to the hot stone or sheet in the oven or place the tin directly onto an oven rack. Spritz all around the oven chamber with a water spray, or place a baking tray with ¼ cup of water on the bottom of the oven.

Bake for 30 minutes, turning once, or until the loaf has a nice golden crust and a hollow sound when you tap the bottom.

100% Wholemeal Loaf

This is best made as a tin loaf. It is a very significant loaf for me. The mum of my school buddy Chris Pain was an avid baker and his home always smelled of this bread. The smell of this loaf will always take me back to that house in Sevenoaks, even 45 years later. There is something about it that is truly comforting and homely.

For the pre-ferment

5 g (1 teaspoon) fresh yeast or 2–3 g (⅔–1 teaspoon) dried yeast
200 g (scant 1 cup) warm water
250 g (9 oz/1¾ cups) strong wholemeal (whole-wheat bread) flour

For the loaf

250 g (1 cup) warm water
350 g (12 oz/2½ cups) strong wholemeal (whole-wheat bread) flour
10 g (1½ teaspoons) fine sea salt
neutral oil, for greasing

Day 1

To make the pre-ferment, combine the fresh yeast with the warm water in a small bowl, mixing until dissolved. If using dried yeast, check the packet instructions – you will either mix the yeast through the flour, then add the water, or you may need to hydrate the dried yeast in the water first.

Place the flour in a bowl, make a well in the middle and pour in the liquid. Mix until you have a smooth paste. Cover and leave at room temperature for 2 hours, then refrigerate for 12–24 hours.

Day 2

Add the pre-ferment to the warm water and mix together.

Combine the flour and salt in a separate bowl, then make a well in the middle and pour in the liquid. Gently bring the dough together.

Once the dough starts coming together, transfer it to the work surface. Don't add any flour. Push the dough into the table with the heel of your hand and knead for 5–8 minutes. The dough will become elasticated, but will be quite wet. Don't be tempted to add more flour.

Form the dough into a round and place it back in the bowl. Cover and leave for 1–2 hours at room temperature. (At this stage, you can leave it to prove slowly in the refrigerator overnight – this will develop the flavour of your bread considerably.)

Release the dough from the bowl – this will gently knock it back, releasing some of the gas and encouraging the yeast to start working a bit faster. Shape it into a loose round shape, then cover again and leave to rest for at least 10 minutes.

Continued next page →

---

2 days
Makes 1 large loaf

Day 1
Preparation – 5 minutes
Resting – 2 hours
Chilling – 12-24 hours

Day 2
Preparation – 15 minutes
Proving – 1-2 hours +
10 minutes + 1-2 hours
Baking – 35 minutes

Lightly oil a 900-g (2-lb) loaf tin (pan). Shape your dough as desired and place it in the tin. Cover with a damp dish towel and leave to prove at room temperature for a further 1–2 hours. You can tell when it's ready by gently pushing your finger into the dough. If it springs back nicely it's ready, but if it leaves an indent it isn't.

Preheat the oven to 230°C fan (475°F/gas 9) or as hot as your oven will go.

If you wish, you can score the top of the dough with a razor or a sharp serrated knife, or leave it as is.

Place the tin into the oven and lightly spritz the oven chamber with water or place a baking tray filled with ¼ cup water on the bottom of the oven. Bake for 35 minutes, turning once, until the loaf has a nice golden crust and a hollow sound when you tap the bottom.

Lazy Focaccia

A high-hydration dough, this starts its life as what appears to be a very sloppy mix, but with a bit of folding and care it becomes a beautifully springy, elastic, pillowy dough. This dough base can be used to create all sorts of bakes with various toppings. For example, fresh herbs, chopped onions, artichoke hearts, tomatoes ... let your imagination go wild. We recommend using a very good-quality olive oil as this really does form the underlying flavour that the focaccia is all about. This has been one of the staple breads of the Bread Ahead range from day one at our Borough Market bakery.

500 g (1 lb 2 oz/3½ cups) strong white (bread) flour
10 g (1½ teaspoons) fine sea salt
6 g (1¼ teaspoons) fresh yeast or 3 g (1 teaspoon) dried active yeast
400 g (generous 1½ cups) water, at room temperature
80 g (⅓ cup) olive oil, plus extra for brushing
sea salt flakes, fresh rosemary sprigs or your favourite toppings

Stage 1

Place the flour and salt in a bowl and combine.

In a separate bowl, add the yeast to the water and mix until dissolved (if using dried yeast, just mix the yeast through the flour mixture). Make a well in the middle of the flour mixture and pour in the liquid, then bring the mixture together to form a loose dough. (If using a stand mixer, use the dough hook attachment to bring the ingredients together.) Use a spatula, dough scraper, spoon or your hand to bring the dough together, mixing for a few minutes until all the ingredients are evenly incorporated. You want a glossy dough with no lumps of flour in it.

Drizzle 2 tablespoons of the olive oil around the edges of the bowl and use a scraper or spoon to gently tease the oil around the edges of the bowl so that is evenly distributed underneath the dough and over the top.

You now need to fold the dough. Place your hands under one side of the dough, pull it up and stretch it over to the other side. Do this from the bottom, then the top and then each of the two sides (this is considered a single fold and will trap layers of air within the dough). Leave to rest for 30 minutes.

Give your dough three more folds in the same way, resting for 30 minutes after each of the first two folds. After the third and final fold, move the dough to the refrigerator and rest for 10 minutes.

Continued next page →

Stage 1

Preparation - 15 minutes
Resting - 1 hour 40 minutes
(split into 3 x 30-minute and
1 x 10-minute rests)

Stage 2

Preparation - 5 minutes
Resting - 30 minutes
Optional holding time - 4 hours
Baking - 15 minutes

Continued →

Stage 2

Preheat the oven to 220°C fan (475°F/gas 9) or as hot as it will go. Lightly oil a large baking tray (pan) with some of the remaining oil.

Gently slide the rested dough into the prepared baking tray. Fold it in half (like a giant Cornish pasty) and massage the remaining olive oil into the surface of the dough, making sure it is evenly covered. Press your fingers into the top of the dough to spread it out to fill the tray. Make sure you press over the whole surface of the dough (this will give your focaccia its dimpled appearance). Top with your desired toppings (except the salt) and leave to rest for 30 minutes.

If you like, you can now hold your focaccia for up to 4 hours in the refrigerator before baking.

Sprinkle the top of the dough with salt. Transfer to the oven and lightly spray the oven chamber with water or place a baking tray filled with ¼ cup water on the bottom of the oven. Bake for 15 minutes or until crispy and golden. Remove from the oven, brush with a little more olive oil, then cool and serve.

Lazy Ciabatta

We call this lazy ciabatta, not because it isn't the real deal, but because we've perfected the method over the years to give novice (and experienced) bakers a method that requires a lot less muscle with great results every time.

400 g (14 oz/3¼ cups) strong white (bread) flour, plus extra for dusting
8 g (1¼ teaspoons) fine sea salt
6 g (1¼ teaspoons) fresh yeast or 3 g (1 teaspoon) dried active yeast
350 g (generous 1⅓ cups) water, at room temperature
2 tablespoons olive oil
polenta (fine semolina), for dusting

Stage 1

Place the flour and salt in a bowl and combine.

In a separate bowl, add the yeast to the water and mix until dissolved (if using dried yeast, just mix it through the flour mixture). Make a well in the middle of the flour and pour in the liquid, then bring together into a loose dough. Use a spatula, dough scraper or your hand to bring the dough together, mixing for a few minutes until everything is evenly incorporated. You want a glossy dough with no lumps of flour in it.

Drizzle the olive oil around the edges of the bowl and use a scraper or spoon to gently tease the oil around the edges of the bowl so that is evenly distributed underneath the dough. Place your hands under one side of the dough, pull it up and stretch it over to the other side. Do this from the bottom, then the top and then each of the two sides (this is considered a single fold and will trap layers of air within the dough). Leave to rest for 30 minutes.

Give your dough three more folds in the same way, resting for 30 minutes after each of the first two folds. After the third and final fold, move the dough to the refrigerator and rest for 10 minutes.

Stage 2

Preheat the oven to 230°C fan (475°F/gas 9) or as hot it will go. Line a large baking sheet with baking paper and sprinkle with polenta.

Heavily flour the top of the dough and the work surface. Use a scraper to release the dough from the sides of the bowl, then turn the dough out onto the prepared surface. Cut the dough into 2 slipper shapes, turn each over once on the floured surface, then transfer to the prepared baking sheet. Cover with a dish towel and leave to rest for 15 minutes.

Transfer to the oven and bake for 16 minutes, then remove and let cool. Serve and enjoy a real taste of Italy.

2½ hours
Makes 2 loaves

Stage 1

Preparation – 15 minutes
Resting – 1 hour 40 minutes
(split into 3 x 30-minute and
1 x 10-minute rests)

Stage 2

Preparation – 5 minutes
Resting – 15 minutes
Baking – 16 minutes

ANATOMY OF A CIABATTA

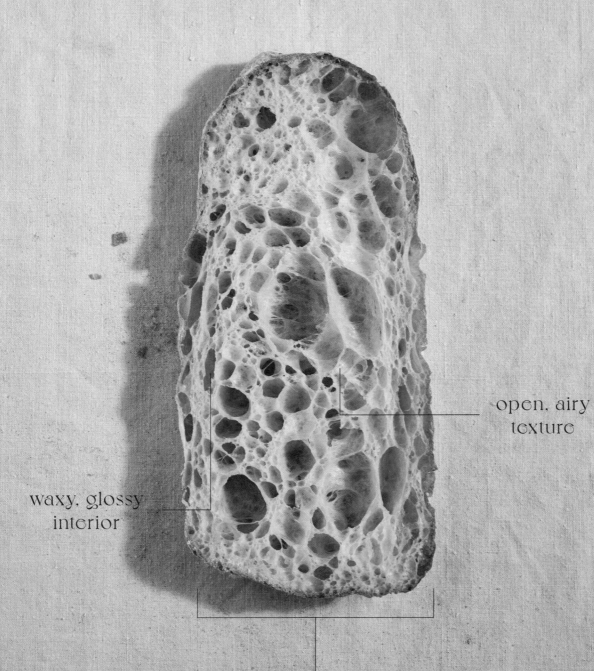

open, airy texture

waxy, glossy interior

thin, crispy crust

Pissaladière

This is a true taste of the South of France, traditionally prepared with black olives and anchovies. The key to this *pissaladière* is not to overmix the dough, it just needs a light touch. Really take the time to sweat the onions properly, this way they will produce a beautiful sweetness and your finished bake will be all the better for it. Enjoy this as much as you would a focaccia or pizza.

For the dough

5 g (1 teaspoon) fresh yeast
    or 3 g (1 teaspoon) dried
    active yeast
120 g (½ cup) warm water
60 g (¼ cup) light olive oil
250 g (9 oz/2 cups) strong
    white (bread) flour
5 g (¾ teaspoon) fine sea salt

For the topping

3 tablespoons olive oil
900 g (2 lb) onions, thinly sliced
2–3 garlic cloves, crushed
2 teaspoons mixed herbs (herbes
    de Provence)
sea salt and freshly ground black
    pepper, to taste
1 heaped tablespoon Dijon mustard

Optional

few anchovies, to taste
handful of black olives
pinch of fresh marjoram

To make the dough, add the yeast, water and oil to a mixing bowl and let the yeast dissolve in the liquid.

Add the flour and salt to the bowl and use one hand to bring the ingredients together into a rough dough. Knead the dough in the bowl with a few folding motions until it comes together in a smooth mass. This doesn't require excessive kneading like many other yeasted doughs. Cover with a damp dish towel or plate and leave to prove at room temperature for 1–2 hours.

Meanwhile, make the topping. Gently heat the olive oil in a saucepan with a lid over a very low heat. Add the onions, garlic and herbs, season with salt and pepper, and gently cook, stirring, for 40 minutes until the onions are very soft. Remove from the heat and leave to cool.

Preheat the oven to 230°C fan (475°F/gas 9) or as hot as your oven will go. Line a 20 x 30-cm (8 x 12-in) lipped baking sheet (tray) with baking paper.

Roll out the proved dough just enough to fit the tray and place it inside. Brush the surface of the dough with the mustard and scatter over the onions (and anchovies or black olives, if using). A sprinkling of fresh marjoram is lovely here, too.

Bake for 15 minutes until the onions are getting a nice roasted colour here and there.

Serve and enjoy immediately, very much like a pizza.

1½–2½ hours
Makes 1 large loaf
Serves 4–6

Dough preparation – 10 minutes
First prove – 1-2 hours

Topping preparation – 40 minutes
Baking – 15 minutes

Milk Buns

This is a super, quick and simple recipe that can be made from start to finish in around 3 hours, or extended as an overnight dough for the more advanced baker. Either way, the results will be delicious. The benefit of using a little milk and butter in your dough is that it forms a lovely soft milky texture and will extend the shelf life. These can be used to make a delicious burger bun or a soft sandwich bap.

500 g (1 lb 2 oz/3½ cups) strong white (bread) flour
300 g (1¼ cups) full-fat (whole) milk, at room temperature
50 g (2 oz) unsalted butter, softened
10 g (1½ teaspoons) fine sea salt
10 g (2½ teaspoons) caster (superfine) sugar
8 g (1½ teaspoons) fresh yeast or 4 g (1¼ teaspoons) dried active yeast
1 egg, beaten (or more milk)

Combine the flour, milk, butter, salt, sugar and yeast in a large mixing bowl. Use your hand or a dough scraper to bring the ingredients together into a rough dough. Ensure it is well mixed and that there are no pockets of flour or butter.

If using a stand mixer, take the dough hook in your hand and gently bring the ingredients together into a rough mixture in the bowl. Then, transfer the bowl to the mixer and attach the dough hook. On a slow speed, mix the ingredients together until you have a dough with no traces of flour or butter.

Transfer the dough to the work surface – don't add any flour. Knead for just a few minutes until it is smooth and relatively elastic. It will be quite a tight dough.

Return the dough to the bowl, cover with a damp dish towel or plate and leave to prove at room temperature for about 45 minutes, or until the dough has doubled in size. At this stage, you can cover the dough and leave it to prove slowly in the refrigerator overnight.

Line a 20 x 30-cm (8 x 12-in) baking sheet (tray) with baking paper or brush it lightly with oil.

Once your dough has had its first prove, release it from the bowl and place on the work surface. Divide the dough into 12 pieces, about 60 g (2 oz) each.

Continued next page →

Preparation – 15 minutes
First prove – 45 minutes
(or overnight)

Shaping – 15 minutes
Second prove – 1–1½ hours
Baking – 12–15 minutes

Continued →

To shape your rolls, there are two methods:

Place a dough ball on the work surface in front of you. With the palms of your hands facing upwards and the inside edge of each hand against the sides of the dough ball, pinch and rotate the dough with the sides of your hands. Between each pinch and rotation, lightly flatten the dough ball and continue to pinch and rotate.

Alternatively, place your hand over the dough ball, cupping the dough lightly. With your hand in a claw-like shape over the dough, gently rotate your hand in a circular motion, applying a small amount of pressure with the palm of your hand on the top of the dough ball as you rotate. This uses the work surface to create a little friction as you rotate the dough.

Place the shaped dough balls onto the prepared baking sheet, leaving a space of about 5 mm–1 cm (½ in) in between each one, as they will expand as they prove. Cover with a damp dish towel and leave to prove for 1–1½ hours until doubled in size (the proving time will depend on the warmth of your kitchen).

Preheat the oven to 210°C fan (450°F/gas 8) .

Brush the buns with egg wash or milk and bake for 12–15 minutes until golden all over.

Crumpets

For best results, the batter should be made the day before and left in the refrigerator overnight to activate the yeast. These can be cooked in either butter or lard, but most important is a low to medium heat to ensure they are fully cooked through. I believe crumpets are one of the hidden gems of the British baking world, especially when oozing with butter.

6 g (1 heaped teaspoon) fresh yeast
200 g (scant 1 cup) warm water
150 g (5 oz/1¼ cups) strong white (bread) flour
2 g (⅓ teaspoon) fine sea salt
½ teaspoon sugar
1 teaspoon baking powder
butter (or lard), for frying

Dissolve the yeast in the warm water.

Add the flour, salt, sugar and baking powder to a large mixing bowl and stir to combine. Make a well in the middle, pour in the yeasted water and whisk vigorously for about 2–3 minutes until you have a thick and slightly aerated batter.

Cover the mixing bowl with a plate or shower cap and leave to stand for 3–4 hours at room temperature. This rest period will help to really develop the flavour and texture of your crumpets. Alternatively, leave the bowl at room temperature for 1 hour, then cover it and place in the refrigerator overnight.

When ready to cook, lightly grease two 9-cm (3½-in) diameter metal rings (or as many as you have) with butter.

Heat a small knob of butter in a large frying pan (skillet) over a medium-low heat. When the butter has melted and started to foam gently, place the greased rings into the pan. Pour 2 tablespoons of batter into each ring – the batter should be about 1 cm (½ in) deep.

After 1 minute, bubbles should start to appear on the surface of the batter. Immediately reduce the heat to low and continue to cook the crumpets for a further 1–2 minutes. When the bubbles start to 'pop', reduce the heat to as low as it will go and cook the crumpets for a further 3–4 minutes. The crumpets are ready when the bubbles stop popping and the surface is cooked all over. The time it takes to cook your crumpets will depend on the size of the ring you use and the depth of the batter, so do look for the different stages of bubbling.

Gently release the crumpets from their rings and serve warm with plenty of butter and jam. These will be just as delicious the next day, toasted to perfection.

About 4 hours
Makes about 5

Preparation – 5 minutes
Resting – 3–4 hours
(or 1 hour + overnight)

Cooking – 5–10 minutes

Sourdough

Sourdough starter

Beginning a sourdough starter is a precious moment that is often the start of a baking path. We began our sourdough starter (named Bruce) in Southwark Cathedral back in 2013, with a full and elaborate ceremony that was in keeping with the way we like to do things at Bread Ahead. Nonetheless, a sourdough can be started at home with nothing more than a jam jar, a little flour and some tap water and will make equally remarkable bread for the rest of your life.

It's quite an extraordinary concept to grasp that the living culture you create will actually live for eternity if looked after with regular feeding and care. The basic principle with a starter is that you are creating an environment in which to encourage natural yeast cells to live and reproduce so that you can use them to bake with. A sourdough starter is a live product, so it will require looking after on a regular basis to keep it healthy.

It is interesting to consider that yeast cells will adapt to being 'fed' at certain times. If we refresh or 'feed' our starter just once a week, its metabolism will basically slow down, producing a slow-reacting starter. On the other hand, if we feed it consistently every 8 hours, we end up with a far more lively, active dough.

For home bakers who refresh their starter once a week , we recommend giving it a refresh (a feed) 8 hours before you are going to bake with it. It's also advisable to leave it at room temperature for this 8-hour period to encourage as much yeast activity as possible.

We run many sourdough workshops at Bread Ahead, as it is the most popular subject we teach to home bakers. A good understanding of a sourdough starter is a key stage of making really great bread. As ever, practice makes perfect.

Starter (White, Rye or Wholemeal)

The basic starter recipe is the same, whether you are using white, rye or wholemeal (whole-wheat) flour as your base. You can use any starter in most sourdough recipes. However, if using a rye starter, it will be wetter and you may need to add a little more flour to your recipe to compensate.

To check on the activity of your starter, it's a good idea to place an elastic band around your jar to see whether it is growing. Pictured opposite are the progress of three different starters (white in the top jar; rye, below; wholmeal at the back) over the course of four hours after feeding.

Day 1

50 g (2 oz/½ cup) flour (use white, wholegrain rye, or wholemeal/whole-wheat)
50 g (3 tablespoons) cold tap water

Days 2, 3, 4 & 5

1 tablespoon flour (white, wholegrain rye, or wholemeal/whole-wheat)
1 tablespoon cold tap water

Day 1

Mix the flour and water together in a jam jar. Cover with a dish towel and leave at room temperature for 24 hours.

Days 2, 3, 4 & 5

On each consecutive day, add the extra flour and water to your existing starter and mix in. By day 5 the starter should be lively, with some bubbling and a slightly alcoholic aroma.

Screw the lid on the jar or transfer the starter to an airtight container and store in the refrigerator.

Use the starter at least once a fortnight. Before using, feed with 75 g (2½ oz/¾ cup) flour and 75 g (5 tablespoons) water, or whatever volume your recipe requires, and leave at room temperature for 8 hours.

Lazy Wholemeal Sourdough

This method is much like the Focaccia on page 28 – the folding part is essential for really developing the gluten. The key is to keep the dough warm throughout the whole process, as this will create a really flavourful and well-developed loaf. I like this approach to baking as it is very gentle and stress free. It may come across as quite unorthodox, but trust me it really works. From time to time we can all break the rules, as long as it tastes great.

150 g (5 oz) White Starter (see page 46)
350 g (generous 1⅓ cups) warm water
400 g (14 oz/2¾ cups) strong wholemeal (whole-wheat bread) flour
8 g (1¼ teaspoons) fine sea salt
vegetable oil, for greasing

Put the starter and warm water into a mixing bowl and break up the starter in the water with your hands. Add the flour and salt and bring together into a rough dough, then tip it out onto the work surface and knead for about 5 minutes until you have a smooth elasticated dough.

Lightly oil your mixing bowl and return the dough to the bowl, cover with a shower cap or a damp dish towel and leave at room temperature, ideally somewhere warm, for 1 hour.

Give the dough a fold (see pages 28–31), cover and leave to rest for a further 1 hour.

Give the dough a second fold, cover and leave to rest for another 1 hour.

Give the dough a third and final fold and rest for a final 1 hour.

Preheat the oven to 210°C fan (450°F/gas 8). If baking your loaf in a Dutch oven (casserole dish), place it in the oven to warm up. Alternatively, lightly oil a 900-g (2-lb) loaf tin (pan).

The dough should have had a total of three folds and 4 hours of resting time. After the final hour of proving, remove the dough from the bowl and shape it according to how you will bake it. Form it into a round if baking in a Dutch oven, or into a standard loaf shape if baking in a tin.

To bake in a Dutch oven, carefully remove the dish from the oven and gently place the dough inside, cover with the lid and bake for 30 minutes, then remove the lid and bake for a further 10 minutes.

To bake in a tin, place the tin onto the middle shelf of the oven and put a tray filled with ¼ cup of water onto the bottom of the oven to create steam. Bake for 30 minutes, then turn the tin around and bake for a final 10 minutes.

Remove the baked loaf from the oven and leave to cool completely before slicing.

Rustic Country Loaf

This is an interesting loaf, as we approach it slightly differently. By using warm water, we accelerate the yeast activity, which enables a quicker fermentation time and less acidity in the bread. Ultimately, we're looking for a really moist, open-textured loaf with a thin, crispy crust. The addition of the toasted wheatgerm gives it a really good nutty flavour.

For the wheatgerm

50 g (2 oz/½ cup) wheatgerm (you can also use sesame or sunflower seeds)
50 g (3 tablespoons) water

For the dough

400 g (14 oz/2¾ cups) strong white (bread) flour
50 g (2 oz/scant ½ cup) strong wholemeal (whole-wheat bread) flour, plus extra for dusting
150 g (5 oz) White Starter (see page 46)
420 g (1⅔ cups) warm water
8 g (1¼ teaspoons) fine sea salt
vegetable oil, for greasing

Day 1

Prepare the wheatgerm. Place the wheatgerm into a dry frying pan (skillet) and lightly toast them under the grill (broiler) or over a medium heat on the hob.

Transfer the toasted wheatgerm to a bowl and cover with the water. Leave to soak overnight.

Day 2

Add the soaked wheatgerm, flours, starter, warm water and salt to a large mixing bowl. With one hand, bring the ingredients together into a smooth, well-combined dough. This is a very wet mix – there's no need to add any more flour, just ensure the ingredients are all well combined.

Transfer the dough to a lightly oiled mixing bowl, cover with a plate, damp dish towel or shower cap and leave to prove for 1 hour at room temperature.

Complete a full set of folds (see pages 28–31), then cover and leave the dough for a further 1 hour.

Complete a second set of folds, cover and leave for another 1 hour.

Place the covered bowl in the refrigerator overnight.

Continued next page →

3 days
Makes 1 large loaf

Day 1
Preparation – 5 minutes
Soaking – overnight

Day 2
Preparation – 15 minutes
Proving – 3 hours + overnight

ANATOMY OF A COUNTRY LOAF

golden and crunchy, thinner crust

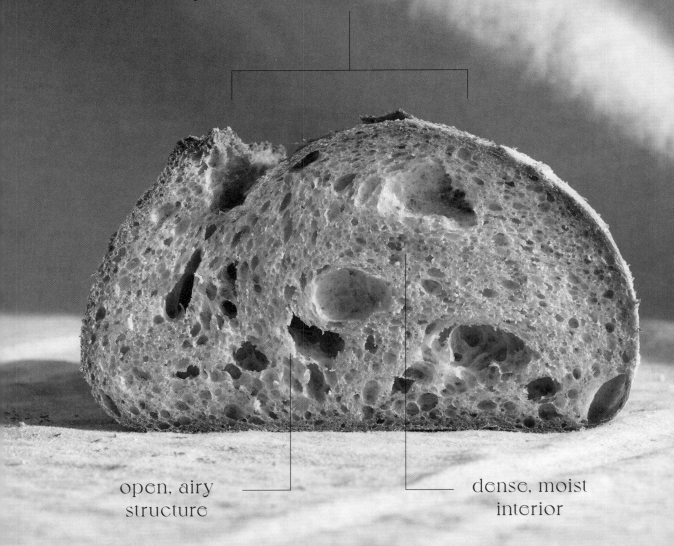

open, airy
structure

dense, moist
interior

Continued →

Day 3

Allow the dough to come up to room temperature (2–3 hours).

Turn the dough out onto a very lightly oiled work surface. Carefully stitch the dough into a loaf shape (see page 20). Alternatively, you can simply fold the dough over in two and pinch the seam together. You want to be careful not to overhandle the dough, it only needs a very gentle shaping.

Dust a banneton with flour and place the loaf into the banneton, seam-side up. Cover with a damp dish towel and leave to prove for 2 hours at room temperature.

Preheat the oven to 230°C fan (475°F/gas 9). Place a Dutch oven (casserole dish) in the oven to warm up.

Carefully remove the Dutch oven from the oven and gently place the dough inside, cover with the lid and bake for 40 minutes, then remove the lid and bake for a further 10–15 minutes to get a really nice scorch on the crust. You may want to turn the oven down a little for the last 10–15 minutes.

Porridge Sourdough

By introducing porridge to the sourdough mix, we create a structure that will support a really high-hydration dough. This is probably a bit more complex as a bread, but really well worth the effort. Once people find this loaf on the shelves of Bread Ahead, they are converted for life.

For the porridge

50 g (2 oz/scant ½ cup) oats (any type)
120 g (½ cup) water

For the dough

170 g (¾ cup) water, at room temperature
35 g (1¼ oz) White Starter (see page 46)
10 g (½ oz) Rye Starter (see page 46)
160 g (5½ oz/1¼ cups) strong white (bread) flour, plus extra for dusting
70 g (2½ oz/generous ½ cup) strong wholemeal (whole-wheat bread) flour
5 g (¾ teaspoon) fine sea salt
vegetable oil, for greasing

Stage 1

To make the porridge, add the oats and water to a saucepan and cook until the water has reduced and the porridge has thickened. The amount of time this takes will depend on the variety of oats you use.

Remove the porridge from the heat and leave to cool to at least room temperature. To cool it faster, spread it over a plate or tray.

Meanwhile, prepare the dough. Add the water and the starters to a large mixing bowl and break up the starters in the water using your hands. Add the flours and bring the ingredients together into a rough dough, then empty the dough onto your work surface and knead for about 3 minutes.

Note: You can also mix the dough in a stand mixer fitted with a dough hook.

Once the porridge has cooled, fold it into the dough and continue to knead for a further 3 minutes until the porridge is well dispersed throughout.

Sprinkle the salt over the dough, then fold it in. You can be quite vigorous at this stage in order to really work the salt through the dough. Continue to knead for a further 3 minutes. It will be quite sticky and loose, but you will feel an elasticity and tension in the dough.

Lightly oil the mixing bowl and return the dough to the bowl. Cover with a plate, damp dish towel or shower cap and leave to prove at room temperature for 2 hours.

Continued next page →

6 hours 40 minutes or 2 days
Makes 1 large loaf

Stage 1
Preparation - 25 minutes
Proving - 2 hours
Resting - overnight (optional)

Stage 2 (ambient method)
Preparation - 5 minutes
Proving - 3½ hours
Baking - 40 minutes

Continued →

Stage 2

After the dough has proved, you can either let the dough continue to prove slowly in the refrigerator overnight or over several hours using the ambient method:

Overnight method

After the first prove, place the bowl in the refrigerator overnight.

The following day, remove the dough from the refrigerator and allow it to come up to room temperature (about 2 hours).

Dust a banneton, or a bowl covered with a clean dish towel, with flour. Shape your loaf to your desired shape and place it in the banneton. Cover with a damp dish towel and leave to prove at room temperature for a further 2 hours.

Ambient method

After the first prove, complete a full set of folds (see pages 28–31), cover the dough and leave at room temperature for 1 hour.

Complete a second and final set of folds, cover and leave the dough for another 1 hour.

Dust a banneton, or a bowl covered with a clean dish towel, with flour. Shape your loaf to your desired shape and place it in the banneton. Cover with a damp dish towel and leave to prove for a further 1½ hours.

It is essential that you keep the dough warm if using this method.

To finish

Preheat the oven to 230°C fan (475°F/gas 9) and place a Dutch oven in the oven to warm up.

Carefully remove the Dutch oven from the oven and gently place the dough inside. Cover with the lid and bake for 30 minutes, then remove the lid and bake for a further 10 minutes.

Day 2 (overnight method)
Resting – 2 hours
Proving – 2 hours
Baking – 40 minutes

Tip

If you only have a white or a rye starter, you can use 45 g (1¾ oz) of whichever you have available.

100% Rye with Seeds

This 100% rye bread is quite unusual in that it is one of the breads I believe gets better with age. For me it's not really an everyday eating bread, it's more of a vehicle for eating smoked salmon, pickled herrings, and even caviar. I think it's best when it's 3–4 days old, sliced thin, spread with butter and topped with smoked salmon and pickles as an open sandwich. We found the addition of seeds to the rye makes the bread more moist. The natural oils of the seeds seep into the bread and make for a much more interesting eating experience.

Seed mixture

5 g (¼ oz/1½ teaspoons) fennel seeds
15 g (½ oz/2 tablespoons) each:
  caraway seeds, golden linseeds
  and poppy seeds
15 g (½ oz/2½ tablespoons) roasted
  wheatgerm
30 g (1 oz/3 tablespoons) sesame seeds
30 g (1 oz/¼ cup) sunflower seeds
30 g (1 oz/¼ cup) jumbo oats
30 g (1 oz/⅓ cup) cracked wheat
170 g (¾ cup) water

For the pre-ferment

55 g (2 oz) Rye Starter (see page 46)
85 g (3 oz/generous ¾ cup) light rye flour
100 g (scant ½ cup) room-
  temperature water

For the dough

240 g (8½ oz) pre-ferment (see
  above)
100 g (scant ½ cup) room-
  temperature water
145 g (5 oz/1½ cups) light rye flour
6 g (1 teaspoon) fine sea salt

To finish

vegetable oil, for greasing
extra seeds, for coating the tin

Day 1

Prepare the seed mixture. Place the seeds, oats and wheat in a bowl with the water, cover and leave to soak at room temperature for 24 hours.

To make the pre-ferment, add the starter, flour and water to a bowl and mix into a smooth paste. Cover with a damp dish towel or plate and leave at room temperature for 2 hours, then refrigerate overnight.

Day 2

Measure out the required amount of pre-ferment and add it to a large mixing bowl along with the water. Break up the pre-ferment in the water with your hands. Add the flour and salt, then gently bring everything together with one hand until just combined.

Add the soaked seeds in their water and use one hand to carefully incorporate the mixture into the dough. It will appear more like a batter than a dough. Cover the bowl with a damp dish towel, plate or shower cap and leave to prove at room temperature for 2 hours. Like the other sourdoughs, it is very important to keep the dough warm, around 24°C (75°F) is ideal.

Lightly oil a 900-g (2-lb) loaf tin (pan) and sprinkle the interior with a mixture of seeds. Alternatively, you can lightly oil a tray and cover it with seeds, then roll the dough in the seeds.

Place the dough into the prepared tin and sprinkle more seeds over the top of the loaf. Cover and leave to prove at room temperature for a further 1 hour (keep it warm), until it has risen by at least 20%.

Preheat the oven to 220°C fan (475°F/gas 9).

2 days
Makes 1 large loaf

Day 1
Preparation – 5 minutes
Resting – 2 hours
Chilling – overnight

Day 2
Preparation – 10 minutes
Proving – 3 hours
Baking – 55 minutes–1 hour

Place the tin into the oven and lightly spritz the oven chamber with water or place a baking tray filled with ¼ cup water on the bottom of the oven. Bake for 55 minutes–1 hour until crisp and nutty brown in colour. Tap on the bottom to check oil the loaf makes a hollow sound.

Cool on a wire rack – it is essential that you let it cool completely before slicing. This loaf will actually mature over time and become much tastier after 2–3 days.

Tip

If using a stand mixer to prepare your dough, use a paddle attachment rather than a dough hook.

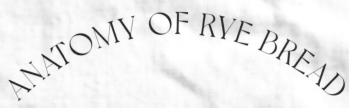

ANATOMY OF RYE BREAD

dark rich
crust

dense and
moist interior

sturdy, robust
loaf

Fennel Multigrain Loaf

This is another old timer of Bread Ahead, and has quite a unique set of flavours. We really recommend it with charcuterie, antipasti, grilled peppers and Parma ham. Although there is only a small amount of fennel, it carries really nicely on the palate and has a gentle, lasting flavour. In this recipe, we recommend fennel, but you could use coriander seeds, nigella seeds, etc., to suit your own taste.

For the seed and grain mix

90 g (3¼ oz/¾ cup) mixed seeds and grains (including fennel seeds, oats, golden linseeds, poppy seeds, pumpkin seeds and caraway seeds)
90 g (6 tablespoons) water

For the dough

150 g (5 oz) White Starter (see page 46)
350 g (generous 1⅓ cups) warm water
400 g (14 oz/scant 3 cups) strong wholemeal (whole-wheat bread) flour
8 g (1¼ teaspoons) fine sea salt

To finish

vegetable oil, for greasing
extra seeds, for coating the tin

Tip

You can bake this in a 900-g (2-lb) loaf tin, but we prefer two 450-g (1-lb) tins, 10 x 10 x 20 cm (4 x 4 x 8 in).

Day 1

Soak the seeds and grains in the water overnight at room temperature.

Day 2

Add the starter and warm water to a large mixing bowl and break up the starter in the water with your hands. Add the flour and salt and bring together into a rough dough, then tip it out onto the work surface and knead for about 4 minutes until you have a smooth, elasticated dough.

Spread the dough out into a square shape and sprinkle the seed mixture over the surface of the dough. Gently fold the dough over to encase the seeds, then give the dough a few more folds to evenly distribute them.

Lightly oil your mixing bowl and return the dough to the bowl, cover with a shower cap or damp dish towel and leave to prove at room temperature, ideally somewhere warm, for 1 hour.

Give the dough a fold (see pages 28–31), cover and let rest for 1 hour.

Give the dough a second fold, cover and let rest for another 1 hour.

Give the dough a third and final fold and rest for a further 1 hour.

Lightly oil a tray and cover it with more seeds. Lightly oil two 450-g (1-lb) loaf tins (pans).

The dough should have had a total of three complete folds and 4 hours resting time. After the final hour of proving, divide your dough into two equal portions, shape each into a loaf and roll in the seeds to coat the dough. Place the loaves into the tins, cover and leave to prove for a final 1 hour.

Preheat the oven to 210°C fan (450°F/gas 8).

Bake for 40 minutes.

Allow to cool completely before slicing.

---

2 days
Makes 2 small loaves

Day 1
Preparation – 2 minutes
Soaking – overnight

Day 2
Preparation – 15 minutes
Proving – 5 hours
Baking – 40 minutes

Raisin Loaf

I refer to this as one of the undiscovered gems of the Bread Ahead range. It has a small dedicated following of the devout. For me, this loaf is at its best when it's a day or two old, sliced, toasted, spread with butter or a bit of Lancashire cheese. The use of the raisin water helps to activate the sourdough and creates quite a unique dough. This is a dough for the more advanced baker, but it is a truly remarkable loaf.

100 g (3½ oz/generous ¾ cup)
    raisins
100 g (scant ½ cup) boiling water
170 g (6 oz/1⅓ cups) strong white
    (bread) flour
60 g (2 oz) Rye Starter (see page 46)
4 g (heaped ½ teaspoon) fine sea salt
vegetable oil, for greasing

Day 1

Place the raisins into a mixing bowl and pour over the boiling water. Cover the bowl and leave to soak for 1 hour.

Strain the raisins, reserving the soaking liquid in a mixing bowl. Set the soaked raisins aside.

Top up the soaking liquid with room temperature water to make it up to 130 g (generous ½ cup). Add the flour and starter to the bowl and bring the ingredients together into a rough dough.

Empty the dough out onto the work surface and knead for 5 minutes. It will be quite a sticky dough, much like a ciabatta, so keep a dough scraper handy to help you scrape the dough back to the middle. Add the salt and fold it through the dough, then continue to knead for a further 1–2 minutes.

Spread the dough out into a square and sprinkle over the raisins. Fold the dough over to encase the raisins and continue to give the dough a few folds until the raisins are evenly distributed. Be careful not to overmix as you want the raisins to remain whole and not break down too much.

If using a stand mixer, use the paddle attachment and mix the dough ingredients for 3 minutes on a medium speed. Add the salt and continue to mix for a further 1 minute on medium speed. Add the raisins, drop the speed down to low and mix until the raisins are just combined.

Continued next page →

2 days
Makes 1 small loaf

Day 1
Soaking - 1 hour
Preparation - 15 minutes
Proving - 3 hours + overnight

Day 2
Preparation - 5 minutes
Proving - 2 hours
Baking - 40 minutes

ANATOMY OF A RAISIN LOAF

well-risen loaf

soft, thin crust

open, aerated
texture

plump, juicy raisins,
evenly distributed

Continued →

Lightly oil the mixing bowl and return the dough to it, then cover and leave to prove at room temperature for 1 hour.

Complete a full set of folds (see pages 28–31), cover and let rest for 1 hour.

Complete a second set of folds, cover and leave for a further 1 hour.

Place the bowl in the refrigerator and leave overnight (this makes the dough much easier to shape the following day).

Day 2

Remove the dough from the refrigerator and form it into a loaf shape while the dough is still cold. If it is still quite sticky, you can use a light dusting of flour on the work surface.

Place the loaf into a lightly oiled 450-g (1-lb) loaf tin (pan), cover and leave to prove for 2 hours at room temperature.

Preheat the oven to 220°C fan (475°F/gas 9).

Bake for 40 minutes.

Leave to cool before slicing. This is perfect served with butter, a good drizzle of honey or some salty mature Cheddar cheese.

Potato and Rosemary Sourdough

This is what we would refer to as a savoury bread, in as much as it goes really well with soups, stews and good, hearty eating. It's better torn than sliced and is full of robust flavours that give you a really memorable eating experience. As with all sourdoughs, it's a long, slow process to get these results.

80 g (3 oz) roasting potatoes, unpeeled
good-quality olive oil, for drizzling
sea salt and freshly ground black pepper, to taste

For the dough

160 g (⅔ cup) water, at room temperature
140 g (4½ oz) White Starter (see page 46)
200 g (7 oz/1½ cups) strong white (bread) flour, plus extra for dusting
1 teaspoon nigella seeds
½ teaspoon chopped rosemary
10 g (2 teaspoons) olive oil
4 g (heaped ½ teaspoon) fine sea salt

Day 1

Preheat the oven to 180°C fan (400°F/gas 6).

Place the whole potatoes into a lined roasting pan and generously drizzle them with olive oil, ensuring they are completely coated, and season with salt and pepper. Roast for about 40 minutes or until perfectly golden and crisp on the outside and soft in the middle (this will depend on the size of potatoes you use – don't be afraid to take them quite dark when roasting, to really develop those flavours).

Remove from the oven and allow the potatoes to cool slightly before breaking them up slightly with the back a spoon or with your hands – you want a few nice big chunks.

Place the water and starter into a mixing bowl and break up the starter in the water using your hands. Add the flour, seeds, rosemary and olive oil to the bowl and bring everything together into a rough dough.

Empty the dough onto the work surface and knead for 3 minutes, then sprinkle over the salt. Vigorously fold the salt into the dough and continue kneading for a further 4 minutes until the dough is smooth and elastic.

Spread the dough out into a square and lay the potatoes over the top, then gently fold the dough over the potatoes to encase them. Give the dough a few folds to evenly distribute the potatoes, but be careful not to overmix and mash the potatoes too much.

Place the dough back into the bowl, cover with a plate or damp dish towel and leave at room temperature for 2 hours.

Give the dough a complete set of folds (see pages 28–31), cover and leave for 1 hour.

Give the dough a second set of folds and leave for a further 1 hour.

Cover and leave the dough in the refrigerator for 8–12 hours or overnight.

---

2 days
Makes 1 loaf

Stage 1
Roasting - 40 minutes
Preparation - 20 minutes
Proving - 4 hours + overnight

Stage 2
Shaping - 5 minutes
Proving - 2 hours
Baking - 45 minutes

Day 2

Remove the dough from the fridge and allow it to come up to room temperature before shaping.

Dust a banneton with flour and shape the dough into your desired loaf shape. Place the dough into the banneton, cover with a damp dish towel and leave to prove at room temperature for 2 hours.

Preheat the oven to 230°C fan (475°F/gas 9). Place a Dutch oven in the oven to warm up.

Carefully remove the Dutch oven from the oven and gently place the dough inside. Cover with the lid and bake for 35 minutes, then remove the lid and bake for a further 10 minutes.

two

Enriched Dough

Babka Loaf

Babka is a fairly new addition to the Bread Ahead range and something I always wanted to master. Essentially, it is a brioche marbled with a rich chocolate filling. It has a lovely moist eating quality that is enhanced by the buttery nature of the brioche and the bittersweet dark chocolate. In the traditional fashion, we generously brush our babkas with syrup, which is a really important part of the process to create a really moist, glossy loaf.

Prepare the dough at least 12 hours before you intend to bake. The dough will rest in the refrigerator, so it's ideal to do this the night before and bake it in the morning.

For the dough

275 g (10 oz/2 cups) strong white (bread) flour, plus extra for dusting
6 g (1 teaspoon) salt
30 g (2½ tablespoons) caster (superfine) sugar
2 eggs
100 g (scant ½ cup) full-fat (whole) milk
8 g (1½ teaspoons) fresh yeast or 4 g (1¼ teaspoons) dried active yeast
100 g (3½ oz) unsalted butter

For the filling

50 g (2 oz) dark chocolate (70% cocoa solids)
50 g (2 oz) unsalted butter
1 egg
50 g (2 oz/¼ cup) caster (superfine) sugar
15 g (2 tablespoons) cocoa powder

For the sugar glaze

100 g (3½ oz/scant ½ cup) caster (superfine) sugar
80 g (⅓ cup) water

Day 1

Bring all of the dough ingredients, apart from the butter, together in a bowl. When combined, tip onto a work surface, and use the heel of your hand to knead for 5 minutes.

Let the dough rest for 1 minute.

After resting, continue to knead the dough, then start to add the butter, a third at a time, until it is all incorporated. Knead the dough for a further 5 minutes until it is glossy, smooth and very elastic when pulled (see Tip overleaf).

Return the dough to the bowl, cover with a plate and leave to prove for 45 minutes–1 hour until doubled in size. Be careful not to overprove this dough – it will rise a lot in the oven.

Knock back the dough, re-cover the bowl and refrigerate overnight.

Day 2

Lightly flour a work surface. Remove the dough from the refrigerator, place on the work surface and leave it to rest while you prepare the chocolate filling and line two 450-g (1-lb) loaf tins (pans) with baking paper.

To make the filling, place the butter and chocolate in a heatproof bowl and melt over a pan of simmering water. Be careful not to let the water get too hot or touch the bottom of your bowl. When the chocolate and butter have completely melted, remove from the heat and stir until well combined.

Continued next page →

---

2 days
Makes 2 loaves

Day 1
Preparation - 15 minutes
Proving - up to 1 hour
Resting - overnight

Day 2
Preparation - 30 minutes
Proving - 1 hour
Baking - 30 minutes

In a separate mixing bowl, combine the egg, sugar and cocoa powder and whisk to a smooth paste. Add the melted chocolate and butter and continue to whisk until the mixture is smooth and well combined.

Lightly flour the surface of the dough and a rolling pin. Roll the dough into a rectangle, about 40 x 45 cm (16 x 18 in). Arrange so the longest side is facing you. Spread the cooled chocolate mixture evenly over the surface of the dough, leaving a 1–2-cm (½–¾-in) border along the side of the dough nearest to you free of the chocolate mixture – this is where you will seal the babka. [diagrams 1 and 2]

Starting at the edge of the dough furthest from you, begin to create a tight roll across the width of the dough, using your thumb and forefinger to pinch and roll the dough towards you. Make sure the seal of the roll is underneath, touching the work surface, and gently dust the smooth top of the roll with flour. Use a sharp knife to cut the dough in half lengthways to reveal the inner layers of the babka. Each of these halves will create an individual babka. [diagrams 3, 4 and 5]

Form a U shape with each length of dough. Starting with the right side, bring this over the left and place down, then repeat, bringing the right side over the left to form a basic plait, as shown opposite. Don't worry about being too neat. [diagrams 6 and 7]

Repeat with the other half of the dough and place each into the lined loaf tins. Cover with a dish towel and leave to prove in a warm place for 1 hour.

Preheat the oven to 160°C fan (350°F/gas 4).

Bake for 26–28 minutes until golden brown.

Meanwhile, prepare the sugar glaze. Place the sugar and water into a saucepan over a medium heat, stirring until the sugar has dissolved. Bring the mixture to the boil, then remove from the heat and set aside. (This glaze will keep well in the refrigerator for several weeks if stored in an airtight container.)

Brush the babkas with sugar glaze as soon as you remove them from the oven and leave to cool in the tins.

Tip

If using an electric mixer, take care that it doesn't overheat – it needs to rest as well as the dough! After the first mixing, let the dough rest for 1 minute, then start it up again on a medium speed and slowly add the butter to the dough – about a quarter at a time. Once it is all incorporated, mix on high speed for 5 minutes.

How to fold a Babka

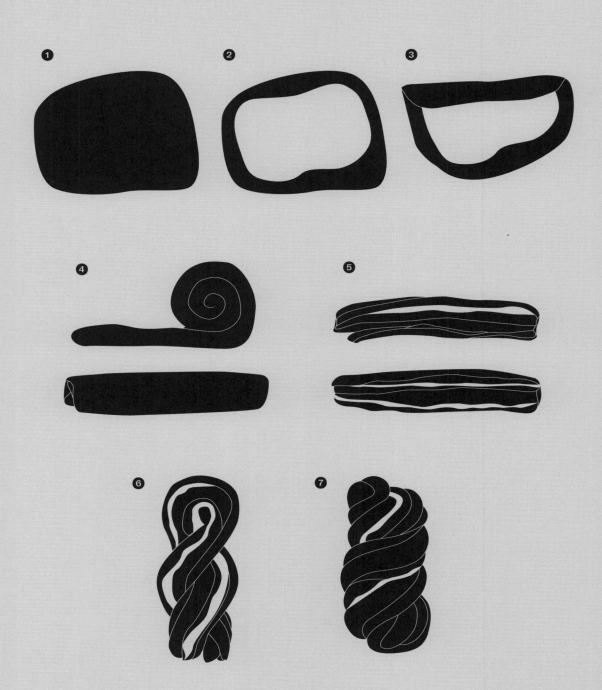

Challah

Learning to plait a challah requires the patience of a saint, as it is tricky. However, once you master it, you'll be amazed. A six-strand plait is a true masterpiece on the table.

We make our challah according to traditional Jewish methods, using oil in the dough, not butter. It is typically eaten on Shabbat and major Jewish holidays other than Passover. Classically, it is decorated with poppy or sesame seeds. To respect the full process, reserve a small piece of the dough and burn it in the oven as an offering.

Prepare the dough at least 12 hours before you intend to bake. The dough will rest in the refrigerator, so it's ideal to do this the night before and bake it in the morning.

300 g (10½ oz/2 cups plus
   2 tablespoons) strong white (bread)
   flour, plus extra for dusting
6 g (1 teaspoon) salt
30 g (2½ tablespoons) caster
   (superfine) sugar
2 eggs
80 g (⅓ cup) water
8 g (1½ teaspoons) fresh yeast
   or 4 g (1¼ teaspoons) dried
   active yeast
50 g (5 tablespoons) vegetable oil

To glaze

1 egg, beaten

Day 1

Bring all of the dough ingredients together in a bowl. When combined, tip out onto a work surface and use the heel of your hand to knead for 5 minutes.

If using an electric mixer, take care that it doesn't overheat – it needs to rest as well as the dough! Once it is all incorporated, mix on a medium speed for 5 minutes.

Return the dough to the bowl, cover with a plate and leave to prove until doubled in size, about 1 hour.

Knock back the dough. Re-cover the bowl and refrigerate overnight.

Day 2

Remove the dough from the refrigerator and place onto a lightly floured work surface. Divide the dough into six equal pieces, weighing about 100 g (3½ oz) each.

Using the palms of your hands, gently roll the dough balls into 40-cm (16-in) lengths (your baking tray/pan should serve as a good guide here). Lightly flour the lengths of dough to stop them drying out or forming a skin while you continue to roll out the remaining dough balls.

Continued next page →

2 days
Makes 1 loaf

Day 1
Preparation - 10 minutes
Proving - 1 hour
Resting - overnight

Day 2
Preparation - 15 minutes
Proving - 1 hour
Baking - 19 minutes

How to plait a Challah

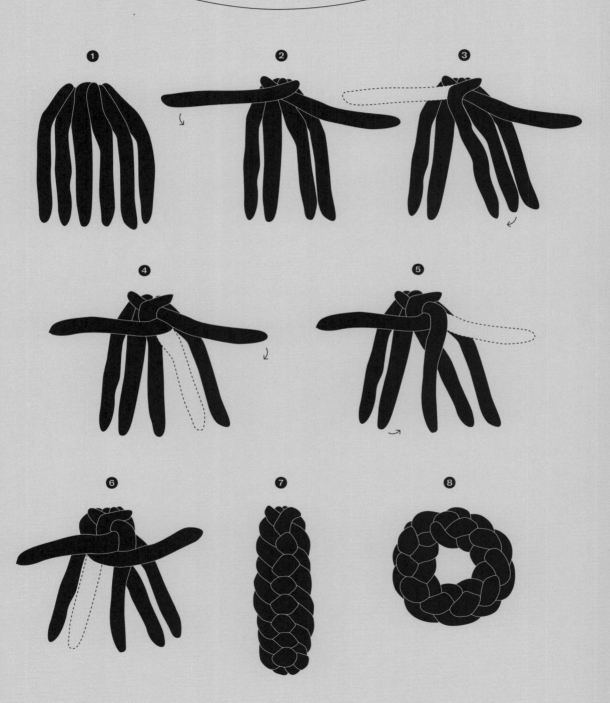

Now to shaping – this is not for the faint-hearted, forming a six-strand plait is not easy, but with practice we promise you'll get there.

First, lay all six strands in front of you, parallel to each other. Join the tops of three adjacent strands together, then do the same with the other three adjacent strands. Join the two sections together at the top, pinching firmly. All six strands are now joined together at the top. [diagram 1]

Separate the strands into four sections. Fan out the outer two strands, and group the inner four strands into two groups of two.

Cross the outer two strands over each other, fanning the ends right out to the sides to keep them apart from your grouped strands. [diagram 2]

* Bring the outer left strand to the middle, grouping it alongside the strands to the right. Bring the second strand from the right to the outer left. Bring the outer right strand to the middle, grouping it alongside the strands to the left. Bring the second strand from the left to the outer right. [diagrams 3, 4 and 5]

Now, repeat the above sequence starting from the *. Repeat until fully braided, then pinch the ends together, tucking them under neatly. If necessary, roll and tuck the ends of the loaf again, tucking them under to make sure they are very secure. [diagram 7]

You can keep the challah as a loaf like this, or you can form it into a wreath shape, pinching the two ends together. [diagram 8]

Place the plaited challah on a baking sheet lined with baking paper. Cover with a clean dish towel and leave to prove in a warm place for 1 hour.

Preheat the oven to 170°C fan (375°F/gas 5).

Generously brush the loaf with egg wash. Bake for 19 minutes until golden brown.

Leave to cool on a wire rack before enjoying.

Frosted Cinnamon Buns

The first time I had a cinnamon bun with frosting was in Phoenix Airport in Arizona, which may seem an unusual place for a gastronomic encounter and yet my life has never been quite the same since. I was overwhelmed with delight. It's everything you want in an eating experience, especially when the buns are still slightly warm and the cream cheese frosting begins to melt. Truly out of this world.

For the dough

50 g (2 oz/½ cup) rye flour
450 g (1 lb/3⅓ cups) strong white (bread) flour, plus extra for dusting
80 g (3 oz/⅓ cup) caster (superfine) sugar
10 g (1½ teaspoons) fine sea salt
300 g (1¼ cups) full-fat (whole) milk
10 g (2 teaspoons) fresh yeast
1 egg
100 g (3½ oz) unsalted butter, cubed

For the filling

180 g (6½ oz) soft unsalted butter
225 g (8 oz/1¼ cups) soft dark brown sugar
75 g (2½ oz/scant ½ cup) soft light brown sugar
3 tablespoons ground cinnamon

For the glaze (optional)

200 g (7 oz/scant 1 cup) caster (superfine) sugar
juice of 1 lemon and 1 orange
1 cinnamon stick

For the frosting

50 g (2 oz) soft unsalted butter
125 g (4 oz) cream cheese
150 g (5 oz/1¼ cups) icing (confectioner's) sugar, sifted
squeeze of fresh lemon juice

Stage 1

Start with the dough. In a large mixing bowl, combine the flours, sugar and salt, and whisk together.

In a separate bowl, whisk together the milk, yeast and egg.

Add the wet ingredients to the dry and bring together with a spatula or dough scraper to form a rough, sticky dough. Turn it out onto a work surface and knead for about 3 minutes until you can feel the dough has become a little more elastic. It won't look like a smooth dough yet. You will need to use a scraper or spatula throughout the kneading process to bring the dough back together.

Add the butter into your dough a third at a time. Place the cubes of butter over the surface of the dough, then knead it in, ensuring it is fully incorporated before adding the next quantity. Continue to knead the dough for 3–5 minutes, using the spatula or scraper to bring it together as before. You will know the dough is ready when it stops sticking to your hand and the work surface. With the dough now smooth, elastic and glossy, place it in a clean mixing bowl, cover with a plate or shower cap, and rest in the refrigerator for at least 1 hour.

Stage 2

While the dough is resting, make the filling. Beat the softened butter, sugars and cinnamon together in a bowl until combined.

Take the rested dough out of the refrigerator and turn it out onto a lightly floured work surface. Use a rolling pin to roll it out into a rectangle, about 50 x 40 cm (19½ x 16 in).

Continued next page →

3 hours
Makes 12

Stage 1
Preparation - 20 minutes
Resting - 1 hour

Stage 2
Preparation - 15 minutes
Proving - 1 hour
Baking - 25 minutes

ANATOMY OF FROSTED CINNAMON BUNS

close, moist crumb

ample and
generous frosting

caramelised base

Continued →

Spread the filling mixture evenly over the dough, leaving a small strip clear of filling along one of the long sides. Brush this clear strip with a little water (this will be used to seal the dough once it's rolled). Roll up the dough lengthways, starting from the long side opposite the clear strip, and gently press the final exposed edge into the dough to seal it. Rest the dough seam-side down for a moment.

Meanwhile, line a baking sheet with baking paper. Alternatively, you can bake these in a 12-hole silicone or metal muffin pan.

Cut the roll of dough into 12 pieces, each about 5-cm (2-in) thick. Carefully transfer them to the prepared baking sheet (or place them in the holes of the muffin pan) and gently press them down so they are each about 4-cm (1½-in) high. Cover with a clean dish towel. Leave to prove in a warm place for about 1 hour until almost doubled in size and touching each other.

Meanwhile, make the glaze, if using. The glaze is optional but it does add a real sweet decadence to the buns. Place all the glaze ingredients in a small saucepan and set over a low heat. When the sugar has dissolved, increase the heat and bring to a boil, then reduce the heat and simmer fast for a couple of minutes. Remove from the heat and set aside.

For the frosting, ensure the butter and cream cheese are at room temperature. Beat the butter in a bowl until completely smooth. Add the cream cheese, icing sugar and a squeeze of lemon juice for flavour. Beat until you have a smooth and creamy frosting. You can chill this in the refrigerator until needed.

Preheat the oven to 180°C fan (400°F/gas 6).

Bake the buns for 15 minutes, then turn the baking sheet around in the oven and bake for a further 10 minutes until golden brown.

Transfer to a wire rack to cool but leave the buns on the baking sheet.

When cool, brush generously with the glaze, if using, then spread over the frosting. You can add a drizzle more syrup over the top, if you like.

Tip

You can use plain (all-purpose) flour instead of strong white (bread) flour, if you like.

Brioche Loaf

Brioche is a central part of classic French baking. It's incredibly versatile as a dough and can be extended to make many different products.
We suggest starting off by making a classic brioche loaf. This recipe has slightly less sugar than most brioches, so it's ideal for eating with pâté, terrines and savouries. Once the loaf is baked, it freezes incredibly well due to the high butter content and makes truly memorable toast or French toast.

500 g (1 lb 2 oz/3½ cups) strong white (bread) flour
20 g (4 teaspoons) fresh yeast or 10 g (3¼ teaspoons) dried yeast
30 g (2½ tablespoons) caster (superfine) sugar
10 g (1½ teaspoons) fine sea salt
5 eggs
25 g (5 teaspoons) full-fat (whole) milk
175 g unsalted butter, softened and cubed

To finish

vegetable oil, for greasing
1 egg, beaten
1 tablespoon sugar nibs (optional)

Day 1

Put all the ingredients except the butter into a large mixing bowl. Using one hand or a dough scraper, bring them all together to form a rough, sticky dough.

Transfer the dough to the work surface and knead for about 5 minutes until you can feel it has become a little more elastic. It won't look like a smooth dough yet.

If using a stand mixer, take the dough hook in your hand and gently bring the ingredients together into a rough mixture in the bowl. Then, transfer the bowl to your mixer and attach the dough hook. On a medium speed, mix the ingredients together for about 8 minutes.

Add the butter into your dough one third at a time. Place a few cubes of butter over the surface of the dough and knead it in, ensuring the butter is incorporated each time before adding the next amount. You will need to use a scraper or spatula to regroup your dough, ensuring you bring all of the dough back together throughout the kneading process. Continue to knead the dough for about 3–5 minutes. You will know the dough is ready when it stops sticking to your hand and the work surface.

If using a stand mixer, continue mixing the dough on a medium speed and add the butter one third at a time, allowing about 3 minutes in between each addition. The total mixing time should be about 8–10 minutes. When ready, the dough should appear smooth, glossy and elastic.

Return the dough to a clean mixing bowl, or leave in the bowl of your stand mixer. Cover with a plate or shower cap and leave to prove at room temperature for 1–2 hours, or until almost doubled in size. Then, transfer it to the refrigerator to rest for 12 hours or overnight.

Continued next page →

---

2 days
Makes 2 loaves

Day 1

Preparation - 20 minutes
Proving - 1-2 hours
Resting - overnight or at least 12 hours

Day 2

Preparation - 5 minutes
Proving - 2 hours
Baking - 28-30 minutes

ANATOMY OF
BRIOCHE LOAF

softer bake
crust

light golden colour

even-textured crumb

silky, buttery
texture

Continued →

Day 2

Remove the brioche dough from the refrigerator and lightly oil two 900-g (2-lb) loaf tins (pans).

Divide the dough in half and form each half into a loaf shape. Place in the loaf tins, cover again and leave to prove at room temperature for 2 hours, or until the dough reaches the top of the tin. The dough should be slightly springy to the touch.

Preheat the oven to 160°C fan (350°F/gas 4).

Brush the brioche with egg wash and sprinkle with a few sugar nibs, if you like.

Bake for 28–30 minutes or until golden all over.

Remove the loaves from their tins and allow to cool on a wire rack.

Brioche Buns with Crème Pâtissière

This recipe is somewhat similar to a Danish pastry in its flavours, but we're using brioche as the base dough. Ideally made the day before, so you can bake them fresh in the morning for a sensational breakfast. They can be made with a wide variety of seasonal fruits – soft fruits, such as raspberries and blueberries, work particularly well, but we also love dried fruits like prunes.

200 g (7 oz/1½ cups) strong white (bread) flour
8 g (1½ teaspoons) fresh yeast
12 g (1 tablespoon) caster (superfine) sugar
2 g (heaped ¼ teaspoon) fine sea salt
2 eggs
10 g (2 teaspoons) full-fat (whole) milk
75 g (2½ oz) unsalted butter

For the crème pâtissière

½ vanilla pod
250 g (1 cup) full-fat (whole) milk
3 egg yolks
60 g (2 oz/⅓ cup) caster (superfine) sugar
20 g (2 heaped tablespoons) plain (all-purpose) flour

To finish

vegetable oil, for greasing
1 egg, beaten
your choice of fruits, for topping
caster (superfine) sugar, for sprinkling
flaked (slivered) almonds (optional)
icing (confectioner's) sugar, for dusting

Day 1

Make the brioche dough according to the Brioche Loaf recipe (pages 84–87) and chill overnight.

Day 2

Line a large baking tray (sheet) with baking paper and lightly oil the paper.

Remove the brioche dough from the refrigerator and divide into eight pieces, each about 50 g (2 oz). Shape the dough into rounds and roll into balls, using the same shaping method as the Milk Buns (pages 36–39).

Place the balls onto the prepared baking tray, leaving plenty of space between them as they will spread out. Cover and leave to prove at room temperature for 1–2 hours, or until each ball measures 7–8 cm (3 in) across. It's important the brioche is well proved, otherwise the fruits and crème pâtissière will get pushed out on baking.

While the dough is proving, prepare the crème pâtissière using the method on page 182.

Preheat the oven to 190°C fan (400°F/gas 6).

When the dough is ready, push a little well into the middle of each roll with three fingers. Put 1 tablespoon of crème pâtissière into each hole and top with your choice of fruit.

Brush the edges of the dough with egg wash and sprinkle with a little sugar, or a few flaked almonds. Bake for 16–18 minutes until medium golden.

Remove from the oven and dust with a little icing sugar. These are perfect served still warm with coffee.

2 days
Makes 8 rolls

Day 1
Preparation – 20 minutes
Proving – 1–2 hours
Resting – overnight or at least 12 hours

Day 2
Preparation – 1 hour 15 minutes
Proving – 1–2 hours
Baking – 16–18 minutes

Hot Cross Buns

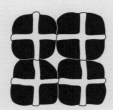

Hot cross buns are the quintessential Easter bake. At Bread Ahead, we only produce them for one month over the Easter period, but we won't blame you if these become a year-round bake in your kitchen. Simply by not adding the cross they become the most sensational little tea buns. Even if they get a few days old, you can slice them open, toast them and enjoy with some farmhouse butter, followed by a nap.

For the buns

250 g (9 oz/scant 2 cups) strong white (bread) flour, plus extra for dusting
3 g (½ teaspoon) fine sea salt
40 g (3¼ tablespoons) caster (superfine) sugar
30 g (1 oz) unsalted butter, softened and cubed
8 g (1½ teaspoons) fresh yeast or 4 g (1¼ teaspoons) dried active yeast
140 g (generous ½ cup) full-fat (whole) milk
40 g (1½ oz/⅓ cup) sultanas (golden raisins)
25 g (¾ oz/3 tablespoons) mixed peel (candied peel)
2 g (1 teaspoon) mixed spice
3 g (1½ teaspoons) ground nutmeg

For the cross mixture

100 g (3½ oz/¾ cup) strong white (bread) flour
pinch of fine sea salt
120 g (½ cup) water

For the glaze

100 g (3½ oz/½ cup) soft light brown sugar
20 g (1½ tablespoons) lemon juice
80 g (⅓ cup) water

Place the flour, salt, sugar and butter in a mixing bowl. Rub in the butter to a sandy consistency. Mix the yeast and milk together until the yeast has dissolved, then add to the mixing bowl. Use your hand or a dough scraper to bring the ingredients together into a rough dough, ensuring it is well mixed and there are no pockets of flour or butter.

Transfer the dough to the work surface and knead. Hold onto the dough with one hand and use the other hand to stretch and fold for around 5 minutes until the dough is nice and smooth. Stretch the dough into a pizza shape and pile the dried fruits and spices in the middle. Fold the dough over to cover the fruit, then gently start to roll and fold the dough until the fruits and spices are evenly distributed.

Place the dough in a bowl, cover with a damp cloth, a plate or a shower cap and leave at room temperature for 1 hour or until doubled in size.

Line a large baking tray (sheet) with baking paper. Place the dough on a lightly floured surface and cut into 65-g (2¼-oz) pieces. Roll each one into a smooth ball and place on the baking tray. Leave plenty of room between them as they will spread out. Cover with a damp cloth and leave at room temperature for about 1 hour, or until doubled in size.

While the buns are proving, make the cross mixture and glaze.

For the cross mixture, mix together the flour, salt and water until you have a smooth paste, then transfer to a piping bag with a 4-mm (¼-in) plain nozzle.

For the glaze, combine the sugar, lemon juice and water in a small saucepan, bring to the boil.

Preheat the oven to 180°C fan (400°F/gas 6).

Once the buns have proved, pipe a cross on the top of each one.

Bake for 16 minutes until golden brown.

Remove from the oven and place on a cooling rack. After 2 minutes, brush with the glaze.

Belgian Buns

I was fortunate to grow up in the seventies and eighties when the high-street baker was still very much a thing, so for me these classic Belgian buns with the cherry on top are symbolic of this era of baking. We adapted the lemon curd to be more citrussy, which balances the sweetness of the icing and the cherry. This recipe is more on the naughty side of things, but deeply satisfying.

500 g (1 lb 2 oz/3½ cups) strong
    white (bread) flour, plus extra
    for dusting
3 g (½ teaspoon) fine sea salt
20 g (¾ oz/2 tablespoons) caster
    (superfine) sugar
280 g (1 cup plus 2 tablespoons)
    full-fat (whole) milk
10 g (2 teaspoons) fresh yeast
    or 5 g (1½ teaspoons) dried yeast
zest of 1 lemon
1 egg yolk
80 g (3 oz) unsalted butter, softened

For the filling

100 g (3½ oz/scant ½ cup) lemon
    curd
120 g (4 oz/1 cup) sultanas
    (golden raisins)

For the topping

250 g (9 oz/2 cups) icing
    (confectioner's) sugar
1–2 tablespoons lemon juice
12 glacé cherries

Stage 1

Add the flour, salt and sugar to a large mixing bowl and whisk together.

In a separate bowl, whisk together the milk, yeast, lemon zest and egg yolk.

Add the wet ingredients to the dry and bring together, ideally with a dough scraper, to form a rough, sticky dough. Turn it out onto the work surface and knead for about 3 minutes until it feels a little more elastic. It won't look like a smooth dough yet.

Add the butter to the dough a third at a time. Place the cubes of the butter over the surface of the dough, then knead it in, ensuring it is fully incorporated before adding the next quantity. Continue to knead the dough for 3–5 minutes, using the spatula or scraper to bring it together as before. You will know the dough is ready when it stops sticking to your hand and the work surface. With the dough now smooth, elastic and glossy, place it in a clean mixing bowl, cover with a plate or shower cap, and rest in the refrigerator for at least 1 hour, but ideally overnight.

Stage 2

Place the chilled dough on a lightly floured work surface and use a rolling pin to roll it out to a rectangle, about 50 x 40 cm (20 x 16 in).

Spread the lemon curd evenly over the surface of the dough, leaving a small strip clear along one of the long edges. Sprinkle over the sultanas, pressing them gently into the curd. Brush the clear strip with a little water and roll up the dough lengthways from the opposite side, gently pressing the dampened edge into the dough to seal it. Rest it seam-side down for a moment.

Continued next page →

3½ hours (or 2 days)
Makes 12

Stage 1
Preparation - 20 minutes
Resting - 1 hour or overnight

Stage 2
Preparation - 10 minutes
Proving - 1 hour
Baking - 25 minutes
Cooling - 30 minutes
Finishing - 5 minutes

ANATOMY OF BELGIAN BUNS

generous filling

single, neat
cherry
on top

even, golden
bake all around

Continued →

Line a baking sheet with baking paper. Cut the roll into 12 pieces, each about 4-cm (1½-in) thick. Carefully transfer them to the baking sheet and gently press them down a little. Alternatively, you can place them in a 12-hole silicone or metal muffin tray (pan). Cover with a dish towel and leave to prove in a warm place for about 1 hour, until almost doubled in size and touching each other.

Preheat the oven to 180°C fan (400°F/gas 6).

Bake the buns for 15 minutes, then turn the baking sheet around in the oven and bake for a further 10 minutes until golden brown. Remove from the oven and slide the baking paper with the buns on top off the baking sheet and onto a wire rack to cool.

Meanwhile, prepare the topping. Sieve the icing sugar into a mixing bowl. Add the lemon juice, 1 tablespoon at a time, whisking to combine (add more lemon juice, if needed – the icing should be a fairly thick consistency).

Once the buns are cool, generously pour over the icing over each one and top with a glacé cherry.

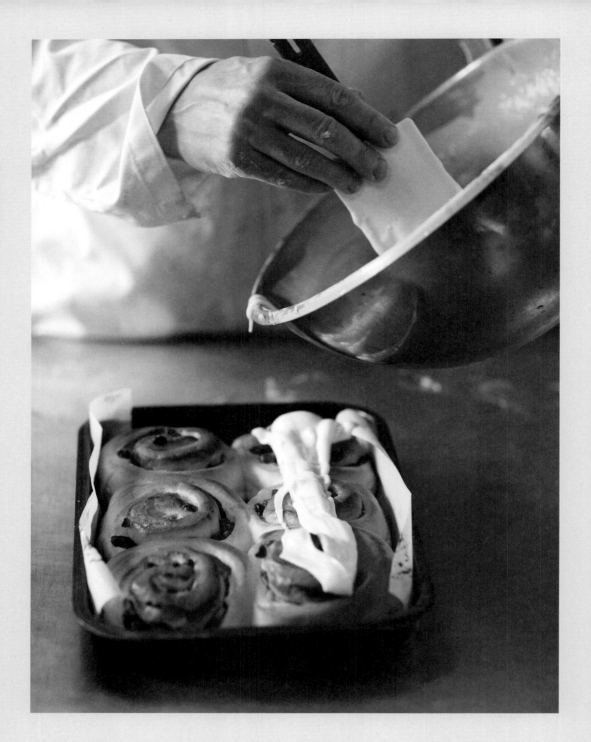

Roscon de Reyes (Rosca de Pascua)

There are several versions of this bake, but we are looking at a traditional Spanish recipe. Similar to a *galette des rois*, Spanish bakeries make this with a ceramic figurine inside. The lucky one who gets the figurine is king for the year. Traditionally eaten on Epiphany, hence the name: King's cake. It is designed to be a colourful and beautiful centrepiece for the festive table. This recipe will make a large roscon to serve 8–10 people, but you can very easily halve the quantities to make a smaller version.

500 g (1 lb 2 oz/3½ cups) strong
  white (bread) flour
20 g (4 teaspoons) fresh yeast
30 g (2½ tablespoons) caster
  (superfine) sugar
10 g (1½ teaspoons) fine sea salt
5 eggs
25 g (5 teaspoons) full-fat (whole)
  milk
175 g (6 oz) unsalted butter, softened

To finish

1 egg, beaten
4 slices of candied orange
  (see page 273)
handful of sugar nibs
handful of flaked (slivered) almonds
icing (confectioner's) sugar,
  for dusting

For the syrup glaze

100 g (3½ oz/½ cup) light
  brown sugar
40 g (scant 3 tablespoons) water
juice of ½ lemon

Day 1

Make the dough according to the same method as Day 1 of the Brioche Loaf recipe (see page 84).

Day 2

Line a baking sheet with baking paper.

To shape the roscon, after the overnight prove, roll the dough into a long sausage shape and form into a ring. Firmly seal the ends together and place on the prepared baking sheet. Brush the ring generously with the beaten egg.

Press the pieces of candied orange into the top of the ring, evenly spaced apart (as if marking the 4 compass points) and scatter over the sugar nibs and flaked almonds. Leave to prove at room temperature for 1 hour.

Meanwhile, preheat the oven to 160°C fan (350°F/gas 4).

Bake for 35 minutes until lovely and golden all over.

While the roscon is baking, prepare the syrup glaze. Combine the sugar, water and lemon juice in a saucepan, bring to the boil, then reduce the heat and simmer for 2 minutes.

As soon as you remove the roscon from the oven, brush it liberally with the lovely sticky glaze. Dust with icing sugar, to serve.

2 days
Serves 8-10

Day 1

Preparation - 20 minutes
Proving - 1-2 hours
Resting - overnight or at least
12 hours

Day 2

Preparation - 10 minutes
Proving - 1 hour
Baking - 35 minutes

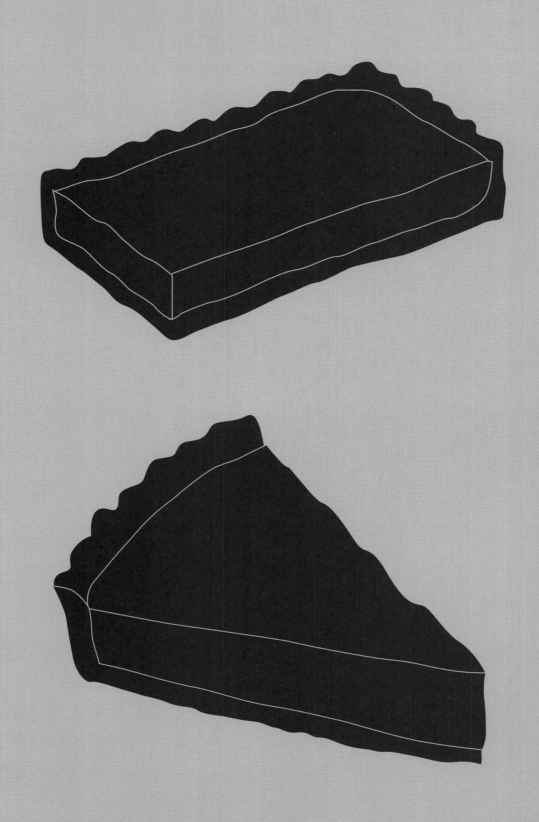

three

Pastries & Tarts

pastry basics

Making good pastry is another example of where practice makes perfect. Here are some key professional pointers that will help to set you off in the right direction.

Start simple

If you are new to the world of baking, I would suggest starting with our 'not so humble' apple pie (page 108). This is a recipe that is really all about the pastry. The apples are, of course, there for flavour and acidity and perfectly complement the buttery, crumbly pastry, but the pastry is the star. Don't worry too much about presentation in the early days, flavour and satisfaction are what this recipe is all about.

Weighing

It is absolutely key to accurately weigh out your ingredients.

Temperature

Our pastries are generally pretty high in butter content. This means they need to be made and rested in the refrigerator, especially if you have a warm home (above 24°C/75°F).

Hand vs. machine mixing

Both are perfectly fine, but for making larger batches of pastry (above 500 g/ 1 lb 2 oz), I would advise using a stand mixer. The key point to remember is not to overwork the pastry. Quite the opposite from bread making, you do not want to develop the gluten when you are making pastry. This is the main reason that plain (all-purpose) flour is often recommended, as it has a lower gluten content, which creates a more crumbly texture in the finished pastry.

Rolling out pastry

Rolling out a lovely, even, round tart shell looks pretty easy, but takes quite a bit of practice. A light, even dusting of flour is important so the pastry does not stick to the work surface. The pastry needs to be kept at an even temperature throughout, so it is important to allow it to adapt to room temperature first, if it has been in the refrigerator overnight. Rotate the dough every couple of rolls and ensure you always have flour under the surface. [photos 1 and 2 on page 105]

Sweet pastry vs. shortcrust

Working with sweet pastry requires a little more patience and a light touch. You'll find the sweet pastries in this book are often more delicate and slightly harder to handle. If your kitchen and/or hands are quite warm, you will want to chill your pastry before rolling out, but do give your dough a few light folds/kneads when you remove it from the refrigerator, to make it a little more supple and easier to roll. If you're new to pastry, try a basic shortcrust first.

Cracking pastry

You may find that your pastry cracks as you roll it. There are two main reasons for this:

Too cold – don't force your pastry when rolling it. When you remove it from the refrigerator, allow it to come up to room temperature. You can also chop it into smaller pieces to help it thaw a little, then bring it back into one piece.

Not enough liquid – different flour varieties will absorb liquid differently. Use your senses to gauge whether your dough needs more water/egg.

Lining a tin

Your rolling pin is your number one assistant when working with pastry.

Gently dust your pin with flour before rolling your pastry over it and use the pin to bring your pastry to the tin. Then carefully place the pastry over the tin and unroll.

Let the edges of the pastry curl inside the edges of the tin, then work your way around the tin, holding the excess pastry in one hand and with your knuckle and forefinger gently pressing the pastry right into the corners of the base of the tin.

Fold the excess of the pastry over the edges of the tin and again, with your knuckle and forefinger, press the pastry into the sides and ridges of the tin, allowing the excess to hang over the sides.

Finally, roll the rolling pin right the way over the tin. As you roll, the pin will cut away any excess pastry. [photos 3, 4, 5, 6 and 7 on pages 105–107]

Blind baking

This is where we need our pastry rolling skills to be really on point. Evenly rolled pastry will cook evenly. Uneven pastry will not!

Before blind baking, I recommend placing the pastry in a nice cold refrigerator or freezer for at least 30 minutes. This will 'set' the pastry around the edges of the tart shell, which will help it to hold in place while it is cooking.

A professional tip for blind baking, when you're getting really proficient, is to start the oven on the hotter side – 170–180°C fan (375–400°F/gas 5–6) – for the first 10 minutes, and then turn the heat down a bit to 150–160°C fan (350°F/gas 4) for the remaining 10 minutes, to cook the pastry right through and make sure the base is fully crisped. There is nothing quite as unpleasant as a soggy bottom. This will also help to 'set' the pastry so it cooks through before it can drop down the sides of the tart shell. Then, follow the recipe as directed to cook the filling.

These days, many bakers and chefs use a double layer of clingfilm (plastic wrap) with baking beans to fill the tart shell before baking it blind. This works very well and creates a nice clean finish to the tart shell. I know that putting clingfilm into the oven can seem a little odd, but it works perfectly. You will have to trust us on this one.

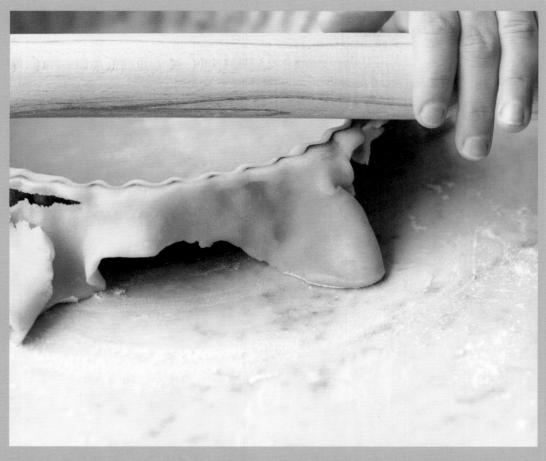

7

Apple Pie

Everybody needs a good apple pie recipe in their toolkit and I truly believe this is the one. I like to use a combination of Bramleys, for their sharpness, and Granny Smiths, which give a more chunky texture. A little ground cinnamon gives lovely flavour and I like to put in a whole clove or two as a surprise for the lucky one who finds it. This is best served with traditional custard or a scoop of vanilla ice cream.

For the pastry

20 g (2 tablespoons) soft light brown sugar
160 g (5½ oz/scant ¾ cup) caster (superfine) sugar, plus extra for sprinkling
250 g (9 oz) unsalted butter, plus extra for greasing
4 egg yolks
450 g (1 lb/3⅓ cups) strong white (bread) flour, plus extra for dusting
pinch of fine sea salt
milk, to glaze

For the filling

4 apples: 2 eating apples (Granny Smith are ideal) and 2 Bramley apples (for a lovely taste) (total peeled and cored weight 600 g/ 1 lb 5 oz)
100 g (3½ oz/½ cup) Demerara sugar, or to taste
1–2 cloves
1 teaspoon ground cinnamon
1–2 tablespoons cornflour (cornstarch) (optional)

To make the pastry, put the sugars and butter in a bowl and cream together until white and fluffy. Add the egg yolks, one at a time, incorporating them slowly to prevent curdling, then sift in the flour and salt and mix until combined.

Roll the dough into a ball and flatten a little. Wrap in baking paper and chill in the refrigerator for at least 30 minutes, but ideally overnight.

Grease a 26-cm (10-in) tart tin (pan) or pie dish, at least 3–4 cm (1½ in) deep, with butter.

Take the dough out of the refrigerator and allow it to soften. Divide the dough into two almost equal amounts: the larger of the two will form the base of the pie and the smaller amount is for the lid. Roll the dough for the base out on a floured surface to 3-mm (⅛-in) thick and large enough to line the tin/dish, then line the tin/dish with it, ensuring that you press the pastry right into the edges. Roll a rolling pin over the top of the top of the tin to remove any excess pastry and add the excess to the remaining half of dough. Wrap the dough in baking paper and rest in the refrigerator until needed.

Chill the lined tin/dish in the refrigerator for 10–30 minutes.

When ready to bake, preheat the oven to 180°C fan (400°F/gas 6).

Take the pie case straight from the fridge or freezer, cover it with baking paper and fill with baking beans, then blind bake for 20 minutes, or until the edges are golden brown.

Remove the paper and beans. If the dough is still a little raw in the middle return to the oven for a further 3–5 minutes, or until golden brown all over.

Meanwhile, prepare the filling. Peel and chop the apples into 1-cm (½-in) cubes. In a bowl, toss the apples with the sugar, cloves, cinnamon and cornflour, if using. The cornflour will help to absorb any excess moisture and prevent the pastry from going soggy.

2–2½ hours plus one optional overnight rest
Serves 8

Preparation – 10 minutes
First rest – 30 minutes or overnight

Preparation – 10 minutes
Second rest – 10–30 minutes
First bake – 20–25 minutes
Final bake – 40–45 minutes

Add the filling mixture to the pie case, then brush the edges with water to help seal the pie lid in place.

Roll out the pastry for the lid to 1–2 cm (½–¾ in) larger than the diameter of the pie. Place the pie lid on top of the case and push down around the edges with your thumb and forefinger to seal the lid to the base. With a sharp knife carefully trim away the excess pastry. Brush the lid with milk and sprinkle over some sugar to create a lovely crisp crust. With a sharp knife, slice a cross in the middle of the lid for steam to escape.

If you like, you can use the excess pastry to make some leaves or decorations for the top of your pie.

Bake for 40–45 minutes until golden brown.

You can allow the pie to cool and then refrigerate overnight to allow the fruit to really set. Reheat for 30 minutes in an oven preheated to 150°C fan (350°F/gas 4).

Bakewell Tart

As with so many traditional British classics, we like to stay as close to this recipe's roots as possible. One key thing that will really enhance your Bakewell tart is using homemade jam, which gives a lovely burst of flavour and perfectly complements the almond filling. This is classically made with raspberry jam, but you can use any jam you like.

For the pastry

softened butter, for greasing
100 g (3½ oz/¾ cup) plain (all-purpose) flour
50 g (2 oz/¼ cup) caster (superfine) sugar
50 g (2 oz/scant ½ cup) fine semolina
100 g (3½ oz) cold unsalted butter, cubed

For the frangipane

150 g (5 oz) unsalted butter, softened
150 g (5 oz/generous ⅔ cup) caster (superfine) sugar
3 eggs
150 g (5 oz/1½ cups) ground almonds
1 tablespoon plain (all-purpose) flour

To finish

2 heaped tablespoons jam of your choice (see page 270 for homemade)
handful of flaked (slivered) almonds

Preheat the oven to 140°C fan (325°F/gas 3) and grease a 20-cm (8-in) tart tin (pan) or deep baking tray with butter.

To make the pastry, sift the flour into a mixing bowl with the sugar and semolina and add the cold butter. Rub the butter into the flour with your fingertips until you have a crumbly but smooth paste.

Transfer the dough to a floured work surface and roll it out to 3-mm (⅛-in) thick. Line the tart tin with the pastry, pressing it right into the edges of the tin.

Prick the base of the pastry case with a fork and bake for 12 minutes.

Meanwhile, make the frangipane. Put the butter and sugar into a mixing bowl and cream together until white and fluffy. Add the eggs, one at a time, incorporating them slowly to prevent curdling, then add the ground almonds and flour and stir to combine.

Remove the tart tin from the oven and increase the oven temperature to 160°C fan (350°F/gas 4).

Carefully spread the jam over the tart base. Spread the frangipane over the top and finish with a sprinkling of flaked almonds. Bake for a further 28–30 minutes until golden brown.

Allow to cool and enjoy with a cup of tea.

1 hour
Serves 8–10

Preparation – 20 minutes
First bake – 12 minutes
Final bake – 28–30 minutes

Blueberry Tart

A Nordic classic and quite unique in its flavours, the rye flour brings a lovely nutty sweetness to the dough and the custard carries the tartness of the blueberry filling. This is a really simple, foolproof recipe. Other berries can be used instead: cherries, blackberries or raspberries all work beautifully.

For the pastry

100 g (3½ oz/generous ¾ cup) plain (all-purpose) flour, plus extra for dusting
50 g (2 oz/½ cup) dark rye flour
100 g (3½ oz/scant ½ cup) caster (superfine) sugar
1 teaspoon baking powder
100 g (3½ oz) unsalted butter, at room temperature, cubed, plus extra for greasing
1 egg, lightly beaten

For the filling

160 g (⅔ cup) sour cream
80 g (scant ⅓ cup) double (heavy) cream
1 egg, lightly beaten
35 g (3 tablespoons) caster (superfine) sugar
1 teaspoon almond extract (optional)
300 g (2 cups) blueberries

Stage 1

To make the pastry, combine the flours, sugar and baking powder in a mixing bowl. Add the butter and rub it in with your fingertips until you have rough breadcrumbs. Gradually add the egg, beating it in until completely incorporated. Bring the dough together and press it into a small disc. Cover the dough with baking paper and chill in the refrigerator for at least 30 minutes (this will allow the gluten to relax and make it easier to roll out later).

While the pastry is chilling, make the filling. Combine the sour and double creams, egg, sugar and almond extract, if using, in a large mixing bowl and briefly whisk together until well combined. Set aside.

Stage 2

Preheat the oven to 180°C fan (400°F/gas 6). Butter a 25-cm (10-in) loose-bottomed fluted tart tin (pan).

Remove the pastry dough from the refrigerator and transfer to a lightly floured work surface. Lightly dust the surface of the dough with flour and use a rolling pin to roll it into a circle at least 1–2 cm (½–¾ in) larger than the tart tin. Make sure you move the pastry around frequently and dust the work surface with more flour, if needed, to ensure it doesn't stick.

Roll the pastry onto the rolling pin and carefully unroll it over the tin. Carefully press the pastry into the creases and sides of the tin to line it, allowing any excess to hang over the sides. Roll the rolling pin across the top of the tin to neatly trim away the excess pastry. Place the pastry-lined tin on a baking sheet.

Tip the blueberries into the tart shell to evenly cover the base and pour in the filling.

Bake for 28–30 minutes until the filling has set and the crust is golden.

Enjoy the tart while still warm, with a healthy drizzle of fresh cream.

---

1 hour 20 minutes
Serves 6–8

Stage 1
Preparation – 10 minutes
Resting – 30 minutes

Stage 2
Preparation – 10 minutes
Baking – 28–30 minutes

Custard Tart

Probably one of the most underrated great British desserts. The trick to a really good custard tart is firstly creating an even tart shell and secondly cooking the custard just right to achieve that lovely jelly-like texture. The pastry needs to be thin and crisp to allow for a generous custard filling. I always grate a little fresh nutmeg on top. There's nothing like it – so simple, yet so delicious.

For the sweet pastry

300 g (10½ oz/generous 2 cups) soft (cake) flour, plus extra for dusting
150 g (5 oz/1 cup) icing (confectioner's) sugar
200 g (7 oz) cold unsalted butter, cubed
2 egg yolks
softened butter, for greasing

For the custard filling

250 g (1 cup) full-fat (whole) milk
50 g (3 tablespoons) double (heavy) cream
1 egg, plus 2 egg yolks
60 g (2 oz/5 tablespoons) caster (superfine) sugar
fresh nutmeg, for grating

Note

If making individual custard tarts, grease an 8-hole muffin tin (pan) with butter. Roll out the pastry to 3–4 mm (⅛–¼ in) thick and cut out 8 circles using a round cutter or saucer as a guide. Carefully pinch the circles into cup shapes and place in the muffin tin holes, gently pressing the pastry into the edges of the cups. Chill for 10 minutes. Blind bake as instructed, then fill each tart with the custard mixture and bake for a final 35 minutes.

For the pastry, add the flour, icing sugar and butter to a mixing bowl. Rub the butter in with your fingertips to rough breadcrumbs. Gradually add the egg yolks, folding them in until completely incorporated. Bring the dough together and press into a small disc, cover with baking paper and chill in the refrigerator for at least 20 minutes. This will allow the gluten to relax and make it easier to roll the pastry later.

Meanwhile, preheat the oven to 180ºC fan (400ºF/gas 6). Grease a 20-cm (8-in) tart tin (pan), 3–4-cm (1½-in) deep, with butter.

Lightly dust the work surface and the surface of the pastry with a little flour. Roll the pastry out into a circle about 1–2 cm (½–¾ in) larger than the tin. Make sure you move the pastry frequently and dust with extra flour, if needed, to ensure it doesn't stick. Roll the pastry onto the rolling pin, then carefully un-roll it over the tart tin. Carefully press the edges of the pastry into the corners of the tin, allowing the excess to hang over the edges. Roll the pin across the top of the tin to trim away the excess pastry. Chill in the refrigerator for 10 minutes.

Place the tart tin onto a baking sheet, cover with baking paper and fill with baking beans. Blind bake for 12–15 minutes, or until the pastry is golden brown and cooked through.

Meanwhile, prepare the custard filling. Pour the milk and cream into a saucepan set over a medium-high heat and bring to the boil.

Combine the egg, yolks and sugar in a mixing bowl and whisk together until well combined. Carefully pour the hot milk over the egg mixture in a steady stream, whisking as you pour. Whisk for a further 2 minutes until the sugar has dissolved and everything is well combined.

Remove the tart from the oven and remove the baking paper and beans. Reduce the oven temperature to 140ºC fan (325ºF/gas 3).

Pour the custard filling into the tart shell/s, carefully return to the oven and bake for a further 60–70 minutes. When the tart is ready it should still have a very slight wobble in the middle. Grate some fresh nutmeg over the top and allow to cool before serving.

1½–2 hours
Makes 1 large tart to serve 8
or 8 individual tarts

Preparation – 5 minutes
Resting – 20 minutes
Preparation – 10 minutes
Chilling – 10 minutes

Blind bake – 12–15 minutes
Final bake – 60–70 minutes for
large, 35 minutes for small

Chocolate Tart

This is a recipe that takes me back to my pastry chef days. Best made with a bitter chocolate that will highlight the various flavours, the shortcrust pastry is buttery and sweet, which complements the chocolate filling, which is both bittersweet and creamy. I like to eat this with thick Jersey cream. Make it several hours before you intend to serve, it's best served chilled, and this will also help to get that sharp, clean cut when slicing.

For the sweet pastry

300 g (10½ oz/generous 2 cups) soft (cake) flour, plus extra for dusting
150 g (5 oz/1 cup) icing (confectioner's) sugar
200 g (7 oz) cold unsalted butter, cubed
2 egg yolks
softened butter, for greasing

For the chocolate filling

200 g (scant 1 cup) double (heavy) cream
100 g (scant ½ cup) full-fat (whole) milk
50 g (2 oz/¼ cup) caster (superfine) sugar
250 g (9 oz) dark chocolate, chopped
2 eggs
pinch of salt

Make the pastry according to the method on page 114. Roll it out immediately or cover with baking paper and chill until needed.

If using a stand mixer, gently bring the flour, sugar and butter together using the paddle attachment on low speed until you have breadcrumbs, add the egg yolks and mix for 30 seconds–1 minute until just combined.

Preheat the oven to 180°C fan (400°F/gas 6). Grease a 24-cm (9½-in) square tart tin (pan) with butter.

Lightly dust the work surface and the surface of the pastry with a little flour. Roll the pastry out to about 1–2 cm (½–¾ in) larger than the tin. Make sure you move the pastry frequently and dust with extra flour, if needed, to ensure it doesn't stick. Roll the pastry onto the rolling pin, then carefully un-roll it over the tart tin. Carefully press the edges of the pastry into the corners of the tin, allowing the excess to hang over the edges. Roll the pin across the top of the tin to trim away the excess pastry. Chill in the refrigerator for 10 minutes.

Place the tart tin onto a baking sheet, cover with baking paper and fill with baking beans. Blind bake for 18 minutes, or until the edges of the pastry are golden brown.

Meanwhile, prepare the chocolate filling. Add the cream, milk and sugar to a saucepan set over a medium-high heat and bring to the boil. Remove the pan from the heat, add the chocolate and whisk until the chocolate has melted and the mix is smooth.

Whisk the eggs and salt together briefly in a bowl. Add the chocolate cream to the eggs and whisk until just combined.

Remove the tart tin from the oven and remove the baking paper and beans. If the middle of the pastry is still a little raw, return to the oven for 3–5 minutes.

Reduce the oven temperature to 160°C fan (350°F/gas 4). Pour the chocolate filling into the tart shell. Carefully return the tart to the oven and bake for a further 20 minutes. Remove from the oven and allow to cool completely before cutting.

1 hour 10 minutes
Serves 10

Preparation – 15 minutes
Resting – 10 minutes
Blind bake – 18 minutes

Filling preparation – 5 minutes
Final bake – 20 minutes

Tips

– Use a sharp knife dipped in boiling hot water to get a really clean slice.

– Use excess pastry to make shortbread biscuits: roll out the pastry to 5 mm
(¼ in) thick and cut into fingers or rounds using a cutter. Bake on a lined
baking sheet for 15 minutes at 180ºC fan (400ºF/gas 6). Remove from the
oven and sprinkle with plenty of caster (superfine) sugar while still warm.

– The uncooked pastry also freezes very well.

ANATOMY OF A CHOCOLATE TART

firm crust

buttery, crumbly
pastry

velvety
chocolate filling

ANATOMY OF A CUSTARD TART

slightly
golden top

jelly-like
custard filling

crumbly, buttery
pastry

Treacle Tart

Treacle tart will always take me back to childhood memories. Yes, this is very sweet, but from time to time that's allowed. We have added orange and lemon zest and juice which gives a lovely citrus note that balances the sweetness of the treacle. The ground almonds also bring a lovely depth of flavour and moisture to the tart as a whole.

For the sweet pastry

300 g (10½ oz/generous 2 cups) soft (cake) flour, plus extra for dusting
150 g (5 oz/1 cup) icing (confectioner's) sugar
200 g (7 oz) cold unsalted butter, cubed
2 egg yolks
softened butter, for greasing

For the treacle filling

600 g (1¾ cups) golden (light corn) syrup
50 g (2 oz) unsalted butter
100 g (3½ oz/1¼ cups) fresh breadcrumbs (brown sourdough is great)
150 g (5 oz/1½ cups) ground almonds
zest and juice of 1 lemon
zest and juice of 1 orange

Prepare and chill the sweet pastry dough according to the method on page 114.

Meanwhile, preheat the oven to 180°C fan (400°F/gas 6) and grease a 24-cm (9½-in) tart tin (pan) with butter.

Place the pastry on a lightly floured work surface and dust the surface of the dough with a little flour. Roll out into a circle about 1–2 cm (½–¾ in) larger than the tart tin. Make sure you move the pastry frequently and dust the worktop with extra flour, if needed, to ensure it doesn't stick. Roll the pastry onto the rolling pin, then carefully un-roll it over the tart tin. Carefully press the edges of the pastry into the corners of the tin, allowing the excess to hang over the edges. Roll the pin across the top of the tin to trim away the excess pastry. Chill in the refrigerator for 10 minutes.

Place the tart tin onto a baking sheet, cover with baking paper and fill with baking beans. Blind bake for 12–15 minutes, or until the edges of the pastry are golden brown.

Meanwhile, prepare the treacle filling. Warm the golden syrup and butter in a saucepan set over a medium-high heat. Remove from the heat, then add all of the remaining filling ingredients to the pan. Stir to combine, ensuring the mixture is smooth and all of the breadcrumbs are well coated in the sticky mixture.

Remove the tart tin from the oven and remove the baking paper and beans. Reduce the oven temperature to 170°C fan (375°F/gas 5). Pour the treacle filling into the tart shell.

Carefully return the tart to the oven and bake for a further 30 minutes.

Allow to cool before serving.

1½ hours
Serves 8

Preparation – 5 minutes
Resting – 20 minutes

Preparation – 10 minutes
Resting – 10 minutes
Blind bake – 12–15 minutes
Final bake – 30 minutes

Lemon Tart

Lemon tart, or *tarte au citron* as it's known in France, is a timeless masterpiece. Enjoy its simplicity and the balance of citrus fruit and sweetness. The key to getting the perfect bake is to take it out of the oven when it is still slightly wobbly in the middle, as the residual heat will continue to cook the filling. Let it go completely cold. I like to serve this with crème fraîche.

For the sweet pastry

300 g (10½ oz/generous 2 cups) soft (cake) flour, plus extra for dusting
150 g (5 oz/1 cup) icing (confectioner's) sugar
200 g (7 oz) cold unsalted butter, cubed
2 egg yolks
softened butter, for greasing

For the lemon filling

zest of 2 lemons, plus 200 g (scant 1 cup) lemon juice
200 g (7 oz/scant 1 cup) caster (superfine) sugar
200 g (7 oz) unsalted butter
3 eggs, plus 3 egg yolks

Prepare and chill the sweet pastry dough according to the method on page 114.

Meanwhile, preheat the oven to 180ºC fan (400°F/gas 6) and grease a 20-cm (8-in) tart tin (pan) with butter.

Place the pastry on a lightly floured work surface and dust the surface of the dough with a little flour. Roll out into a circle about 1–2 cm (½–¾ in) larger than the tart tin. Make sure you move the pastry frequently and dust the work surface with extra flour, if needed, to ensure it doesn't stick. Roll the pastry onto the rolling pin, then carefully un-roll it over the tart tin. Carefully press the edges of the pastry into the corners of the tin, allowing the excess to hang over the edges. Roll the pin across the top of the tin to trim away the excess pastry. Chill in the refrigerator for 10 minutes.

Place the tart tin onto a baking sheet, cover with baking paper and fill with baking beans. Blind bake for 18 minutes, or until the edges of the pastry are golden brown.

Meanwhile, prepare the lemon filling. Put the lemon zest and juice, sugar and butter into a saucepan set over a medium-high heat and bring to the boil.

In a mixing bowl, whisk together the eggs and yolks until well combined. Carefully pour the hot lemon mixture over the eggs in a steady stream, whisking as you pour. Return the mixture to the pan and cook very slowly on the lowest heat for 3 minutes until thickened. Strain the mixture through a sieve (fine-mesh strainer) to remove the lemon zest.

Remove the tart from the oven and remove the baking paper and beans. Reduce the oven temperature to 140ºC fan (325°F/gas 3). Pour the lemon filling into the tart shell.

Carefully return the tart to the oven and bake for a further 40 minutes. When it is ready, it should still have a very slight wobble in the middle.

Allow to cool for about 2 hours before serving.

1 hour 35 minutes
Serves 8

Preparation – 5 minutes
Resting – 18 minutes

Preparation – 10 minutes
Resting – 10 minutes
Blind bake – 18 minutes
Final bake – 40 minutes

Pumpkin Pie

I've tried many pumpkin pies in my time and often found them overwhelmingly sweet. I have created this slightly more savoury version, which I love. It's a lovely thing to bake for Thanksgiving to mark the occasion and enjoy seasonal produce at its best. Please feel free to mix and match the spices to your taste. Wonderful on its own, but a good dollop of freshly whipped cream cuts through the sweetness of the pie beautifully.

1 egg yolk, beaten, for brushing

For the pastry

4 teaspoons soft light brown sugar
100 g (3½ oz/scant ½ cup) caster (superfine) sugar
170 g (6 oz) cold unsalted butter, cubed, plus extra for greasing
3 egg yolks
300 g (10½ oz/generous 2 cups) strong white (bread) flour, plus extra for dusting
pinch of fine sea salt

For the filling

400 g (14 oz) pumpkin purée (see Tip overleaf)
2 eggs
180 g (¾ cup) double (heavy) cream
120 g (½ cup) full-fat (whole) milk
140 g (4½ oz/⅔ cup) caster (superfine) sugar
1 teaspoon ground cinnamon
½ teaspoon ground ginger
½ teaspoon ground nutmeg
¼ teaspoon ground cardamom
½ teaspoon salt

Stage 1

To make the pastry, put the sugars and butter into a large bowl and cream together until white and fluffy. Add the egg yolks, one at a time, incorporating them slowly to prevent curdling, then sift in the flour and salt and mix until combined.

Roll the dough into a ball and flatten a little. Wrap in baking paper and chill in the refrigerator for at least 30 minutes, ideally overnight.

Stage 2

Take the pastry out of the refrigerator and allow it to soften a little.

Butter and flour a 22–24-cm (9–9½-in) loose-bottomed tart tin (pan), at least 3–4-cm (1½-in) deep.

On a lightly floured work surface, gently press the pastry out using a rolling pin just to soften it a little, then roll it out to 3 mm (⅛ in) thick and at least 2 cm (¾ in) larger than the tart tin, rotating the pastry by a quarter turn as you go to get an even thickness. Roll up the pastry onto the rolling pin and unroll over the prepared tin. Carefully press the pastry into the creases and sides of the tin to line it, allowing any excess to hang over the sides. Roll the rolling pin across the top of the tin to neatly trim away the excess pastry. Chill in the refrigerator for a further 10–30 minutes.

Meanwhile, preheat the oven to 180°C fan (400°F/gas 6) and prepare the filling.

This step is optional: Warm the pumpkin purée in a dry frying pan (skillet) over a medium heat, stirring occasionally, for about 10 minutes. This will remove any excess moisture but will also gently caramelise the pumpkin.

Continued next page →

2¼–3 hours
Serves 8–10

Stage 1
Preparation - 10 minutes
Resting - 30 minutes or overnight

Stage 2
Preparation - 20-40 minutes
Blind baking - 17-20 minutes
Cooling - up to 30 minutes
Final baking - 30-35 minutes

Place the pumpkin purée in a large mixing bowl. Add the eggs, cream, milk and sugar and whisk together. Add the ground spices and salt and whisk until thoroughly combined.

Remove the tart shell from the refrigerator, line it with baking paper and fill with baking beans. Bake in the oven for 12–15 minutes, or until the edges are golden brown, then remove the paper and beans and bake for a further 5 minutes, or until golden brown all over.

Remove from the oven and brush the blind-baked tart shell with the beaten egg yolk (to seal any holes or cracks in the case). Leaving it in the tin, transfer to a wire rack and leave to cool completely.

Reduce the oven temperature to 150°C fan (350°F/gas 4).

Place the tart tin on a baking sheet and pour the filling into the cooled tart shell. Bake for a further 30–35 minutes until just set on top – you don't want any cracks to appear on your pie filling. Remove from the oven and allow to cool before slicing and serving.

You may want to reduce the quantity of sugar in the filling to suit your own taste – this may also depend on the sweetness of your purée.

Tip

To make your own pumpkin purée, you'll need 1 small pumpkin or squash. Slice it in half and remove and discard the seeds and stringy flesh, then chop into wedges and halve them widthways. Place the pumpkin pieces on a baking sheet and sprinkle over a few teaspoons of sugar and ground cinnamon. Bake at 150°C (350°F/gas 4) for 2 hours until the flesh has softened. Remove from the oven and leave to cool. Once cooled, scrape the softened pumpkin flesh from the skins using a spoon or fork, and mash.

Herby Mushroom Buckwheat Tart

Feel free to play with the components of this recipe. The mushrooms, for example, can be replaced with artichoke hearts and the Cheddar with a hard goat's cheese. Ultimately, this is a really wholesome and satisfying bake. The pie crust can be made gluten-free very easily, simply swap the plain (all-purpose) flour for a gluten-free version.

For the pastry

60 g (2 oz/½ cup) buckwheat flour
120 g (4 oz/1 cup) plain (all-purpose) flour
1 teaspoon fine sea salt
110 g (3¾ oz) cold unsalted butter, cubed
70 g (2½ oz) mature Cheddar cheese, grated
1 teaspoon finely chopped fresh rosemary (optional)
120 g (½ cup) cold water

For the filling

20 g (¾ oz) unsalted butter
1 onion, finely sliced
2 garlic cloves, crushed
250 g (9 oz) mushrooms, finely sliced
2 teaspoons fresh thyme leaves
225 g (1 cup) double (heavy) cream
3 eggs, plus 1 yolk
50 g (2 oz) Parmesan cheese, grated (optional)
pinch of cayenne pepper (optional)
salt and freshly ground black pepper

Stage 1

To make the pastry, combine the flours and salt in a medium mixing bowl. Add the butter and rub it in with your fingertips, keeping the mixture aerated and light, until it resembles breadcrumbs. Add the grated cheese and rosemary and mix to combine. Slowly add the cold water in 2–3 additions (you might not need all of it) and mix with a dough scraper or by hand until the dough just comes together, adding more water as needed. The dough should be a little bit sticky but holding together.

Transfer the dough to the work surface and knead gently – don't overdo it or you'll end up with a greasy dough. Pat the dough out into a circle, wrap with baking paper and chill in the refrigerator for about 30 minutes (10 minutes if using gluten-free flour).

Meanwhile, make the filling. Melt half of the butter in a frying pan (skillet) over a low–medium heat. Add the onion and sweat for 8–10 minutes until soft but not brown. Add the garlic and stir for 1 minute, then transfer the mixture to a bowl and set aside to cool.

Melt the remaining butter in the same pan. Add the mushrooms and fry until starting to brown, then add the thyme leaves and season with salt and pepper. Continue to cook until all the juices have been re-absorbed, then set aside to cool.

Continued next page →

2-2½ hours
Serves 8

Stage 1

Preparation - 15 minutes
Resting - 10-30 minutes

Stage 2

Preparation - 25 minutes
Blind baking - 25-30 minutes
Cooling - up to 30 minutes
Final assembly - 5 minutes
Final baking - 30 minutes

Continued →

Stage 2

When you are ready to bake, butter a 22–24-cm (9–9½-in) loose-bottomed fluted tart tin (pan).

Remove the pastry dough from the refrigerator and transfer to a lightly floured work surface. Lightly dust the surface of the dough with flour and use a rolling pin to roll it into a circle at least 1–2 cm (½–¾ in) larger than the tart tin. Make sure you move the pastry around frequently and dust the work surface with more flour, if needed, to ensure it doesn't stick. Don't worry if the pastry cracks slightly – you can gently press it back together.

Gently lift the pastry into the tart tin and gently press it into the sides. Don't worry if it breaks up a little – just patch it back together, making sure you have no holes in the pastry. Trim off any excess. Chill in the refrigerator for 10–15 minutes (this should prevent the pastry from shrinking when you bake it).

Meanwhile, preheat the oven to 180°C fan (400°F/gas 6).

Remove the tart shell from the refrigerator, line it with baking paper and fill with baking beans. Bake in the oven for 20 minutes, then remove the paper and beans and bake for a further 5–10 minutes until the base looks dry. Transfer to a wire rack and leave to cool completely.

Place the blind-baked tart shell on a baking sheet. Pour in the onion and garlic mixture and spread evenly over the base of the pastry.

Whisk the cream, eggs and egg yolk in a bowl. Add the mushroom mixture and most of the grated Parmesan. Season with salt and pepper and add a pinch of cayenne pepper, if using. Taste and adjust the seasoning as necessary, then pour into the tart shell.

Sprinkle the remaining Parmesan over the tart and bake for 30 minutes or until the filling is set and the top is lightly browned.

Tips

Ensure the butter is cold – you don't want it to melt into the flour. The dough will keep in the refrigerator for a couple of days or you can freeze it for up to 3 months.

Parmesan and Spinach Tart

This is one from my pastry chef days, when I worked in the kitchen of Quaglino's back in 1996. It is best prepared the day before you intend to serve it, and is delicious served warm or cold. We used to serve it with a simple green salad with some chopped shallots.

For the shortcrust pastry

225 g (8 oz/1¾ cups) plain (all-purpose) flour, plus extra for dusting
100 g (3½ oz) cold unsalted butter, diced, plus extra for greasing
pinch of fine sea salt
1 egg yolk
1–2 tablespoons cold water, or more as needed

For the filling

20 g (¾ oz) unsalted butter
300 g (10½ oz) fresh leaf spinach (not baby spinach)
125 g (½ cup) full-fat (whole) milk
125 g (½ cup) double (heavy) cream
125 g (4 oz/½ cup) mascarpone
2 eggs, plus 2 egg yolks
125 g (4 oz/2 cups) freshly grated Parmesan
sea salt and freshly ground black pepper

Stage 1

To make the pastry, add the flour, butter and salt to a large mixing bowl. Rub the butter in with your fingertips until you have rough breadcrumbs. Add the egg yolk and cold water and bring the dough together with one hand. Add more water as needed, just 1 tablespoon at a time. Shape the pastry into a disc, wrap it in baking paper and chill in the refrigerator for at least 30 minutes, but ideally 2–4 hours.

Stage 2

Preheat the oven to 180°C fan (400°F/gas 6). Grease a 24-cm (9½-in) tart tin (pan) with butter.

Place the pastry on a lightly floured work surface and dust the dough with a little flour. Roll out to 1–2 cm (½–¾ in) larger than the tart tin. Move the pastry frequently and dust with extra flour, if needed. Line the tin with the pastry (see method on page 104). Chill for 10 minutes.

Meanwhile, prepare the filling. Melt the butter in a large saucepan over a medium heat. When it begins to foam, add the spinach and cook until it has wilted completely. Remove from the heat and spread over a tray to cool, then transfer it to a sieve (strainer) to drain for 10 minutes.

Place the tart tin onto a baking sheet, cover with baking paper and fill with baking beans. Blind bake for 12–15 minutes, or until the edges of the pastry are golden brown.

To finish the filling, add the milk, cream and mascarpone to a mixing bowl and whisk together until well combined. Add the eggs and yolks, season with salt and pepper and whisk together. Add the grated Parmesan and combine, then add the drained spinach and fold together.

Remove the tart from the oven and remove the baking paper and beans. Reduce the oven temperature to 160°C fan (350°F/gas 4). Pour the filling into the tart shell, carefully return the tart to the oven and bake for a further 35–40 minutes until slightly golden and crisp on top.

Allow to cool, then cover and refrigerate to firm up before serving.

2–5½ hours
Serves 8

Stage 1

Preparation – 10 minutes
Resting – 30 minutes–4 hours

Stage 2

Preparation – 25 minutes
Resting – 10 minutes
Blind baking – 12–15 minutes
Final baking – 35–40 minutes

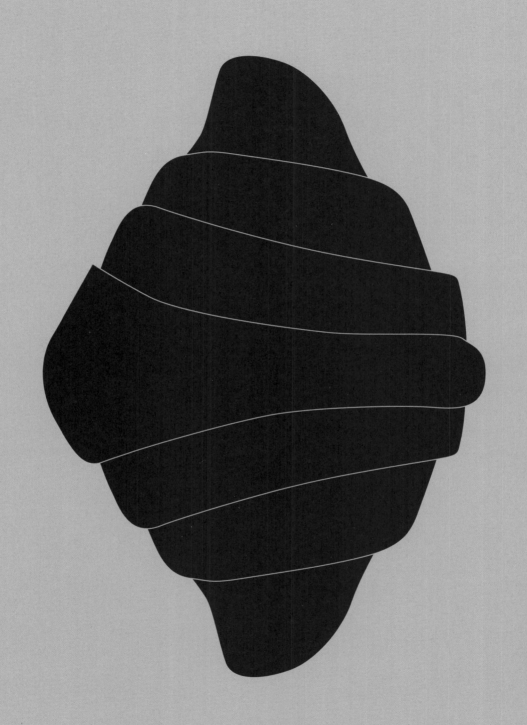

four

Laminated Pastry

Basic Puff Pastry and How to Laminate It

Puff pastry is such a great vehicle for sweet and savoury flavours, it is worth taking the time to make your own. It is a joy to master this technique. If you are going to cut corners and used ready-made pastry, brush a little butter over the pastry for an added hit of flavour.

500 g (1 lb 2 oz/3½ cups) strong white (bread) flour, plus extra for dusting
8 g (1¼ teaspoons) fine sea salt
125 g (4 oz) cold unsalted butter, diced
225 g (scant 1 cup) cold water
10 g (2 teaspoons) white wine vinegar

To finish

375 g (13 oz) unsalted butter, slightly softened

Stage 1

Place the flour, salt and diced cold butter in the bowl of a stand mixer fitted with the beater attachment. Mix on slow speed until the mixture looks like fine breadcrumbs.

Change the attachment to the dough hook. Add the cold water and vinegar to the flour mixture, and mix on medium speed for about 2 minutes. The dough should feel nice and pliable.

Alternatively, place the flour, salt and diced cold butter in a bowl and rub the butter into the flour with your fingertips until the mixture looks like fine breadcrumbs. Add the cold water and vinegar and mix together until a dough is formed.

Take the dough out of the bowl, wrap it in clingfilm (plastic wrap) and rest it in the refrigerator for at least 2 hours, but ideally overnight.

Stage 2

An hour before you take the dough from the refrigerator, use a rolling pin to gently pound the butter between two pieces of baking paper to make it square and flat, about 5-mm (¼-in) thick. Place the butter back into the refrigerator for 40 minutes (it's important that the dough and butter are the same temperature). [see photos 1 and 2]

Place the chilled dough onto a lightly floured work surface and roll it out to a 25-cm (10-in) square. Turn the dough so it looks like a diamond, then roll each corner out so you have a cross shape with four thin flaps and a slightly raised square of dough in the middle. [photo 3]

Place the butter in the middle of the dough, then start to encase it. Fold the top and bottom flaps over to enclose the dough, pulling them slightly so they cover it as much as possible. Then pull the side flaps over, so the butter is fully enclosed as if in an envelope. Tap the dough gently with the side of the rolling pin to help seal it. [photos 4, 5 and 6]

Continued next page →

12 hours or
overnight plus 10 hours
Makes 1.25 kg (2 lb 13 oz)

Stage 1
Preparation – 10 minutes
Chilling – 2 hours or overnight

Stage 2
Lamination – 30 minutes
Chilling – 3 x 3-hour stages

Continued →

With the seam running top to bottom, roll the dough out into a long rectangular shape, about 25 cm (10 in) wide and 70 cm (27 in) long. Make sure all the sides are straight. With one of the shorter sides nearest you, fold it into thirds, first bottom to middle, then top to bottom. This finishes the first 'turn'. [photos 7 and 8]

Turn the pastry so that the seam or join is always on the left and roll it out again, before folding just as before. This is the second turn. [photos 9, 10 and 11]

Wrap the pastry in clingfilm (plastic wrap) and place in the refrigerator to rest for 3 hours.

Repeat another two turns, as above, again resting for 3 hours.

Finally, complete another two turns so that you have completed six turns in total. Rest for a final 3 hours. [photo 12]

Your pastry is now ready to use.

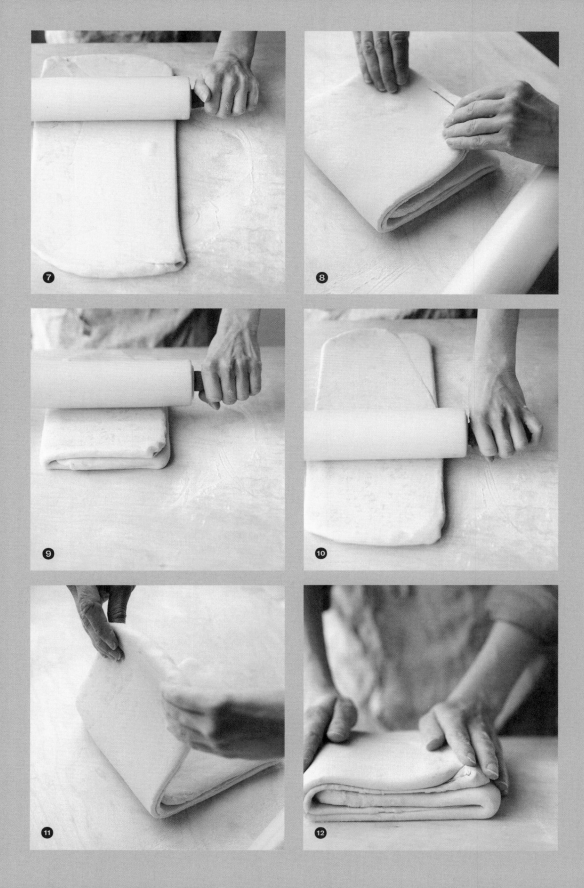

Eccles Cakes

I can never eat just one Eccles cake. It's a strange thing, I always mean to have just one but always end up having three, and then immediately regret it. The Eccles cake mix is best made in advance and kept in the refrigerator so that the currants get the chance to absorb the butter and spices. They can be fully made up and frozen in a raw state for several months and keep perfectly well. It's important to score them three times on top, which symbolises the Father, Son and Holy Ghost, if we are to do things properly.

750 g (1 lb 10 oz) Puff Pastry
   (see pages 134–137)
plain (all-purpose) flour, for dusting
1 egg, beaten, for the egg wash
Demerara sugar, for sprinkling

For the filling

125 g (4 oz) unsalted butter, softened
90 g (3¼ oz/½ cup) soft dark
   brown sugar
25 g (1 oz/2 tablespoons) soft light
   brown sugar
25 g (1 oz/2 tablespoons)
   Demerara sugar
250 g (9 oz/1⅔ cups) currants
juice of 1 lemon
pinch of fine sea salt
2 g (1 teaspoon) ground allspice
2 g (1 teaspoon) ground nutmeg
2 g (1 teaspoon) ground cinnamon
2 g (1 teaspoon) ground mixed spice

Start with the filling. Melt the butter in a saucepan over a medium heat – be careful not to let it bubble.

In a large bowl, mix all the remaining filling ingredients together with the melted butter until evenly incorporated, then chill in the refrigerator for about 2 hours until the mixture solidifies.

Once chilled, roll the mixture into 14 balls, each about 40 g (1½ oz), and flatten them down so that each resembles an ice-hockey puck. Chill for a further 1 hour to firm up a little more.

Roll out the pastry on a lightly floured surface to 1.5-cm (¾-in) thick. Cut 14 discs out of the pastry using a 7-cm (2¾-in) round pastry cutter. Place a piece of the chilled filling mixture in the middle of each pastry disc. Dip your finger into a cup of water and run it around the outside edge of each pastry disc, then pull up the sides of the pastry to cover the filling. Seal together so that no filling is showing. Place them seam-side down on a baking sheet lined with baking paper, leaving some space between them, and gently press the cakes down with the palm of your hand to flatten them a little. Chill in the refrigerator for 1 hour.

Preheat the oven to 180°C fan (400°F/gas 6).

Take your Eccles cakes out of the refrigerator and egg wash them generously all over. Slash the top of each one three times with a sharp knife, then sprinkle them with sugar and bake for 35–40 minutes until golden brown and oozing molten caramel deliciousness.

Leave to cool, and serve with a wedge of cheese, or simply with a mug of tea.

2 hours
Makes 14

Preparation – 20 minutes
Chilling – 4 hours

Blind baking – 16 minutes
Final baking – 45 minutes

Apple Turnovers

A lovely, simple introduction to working with puff pastry, and also a great way to use pastry scraps. Be careful not to put in too much apple filling, as it can leak out and burn. This recipe can also be adapted for other fruits, such as pears, apricots or cherries.

500 g (1 lb 2 oz) Puff Pastry
    (see pages 134–137)
plain (all-purpose) flour, for dusting
1 egg, beaten
Demerara sugar, for sprinkling

For the stewed apple filling

700 g (1 lb 9 oz) eating apples of
    choice, peeled, cored and diced
    into 1-cm (½-in) cubes
30 g (1 oz) unsalted butter
50 g (2 oz/¼ cup) caster (superfine)
    sugar
1 teaspoon ground cinnamon
1 teaspoon vanilla extract

To prepare the stewed apple filling, add the diced apple, butter, sugar, cinnamon and vanilla extract to a saucepan set over a medium heat. Cook the apples down until soft, stirring occasionally to ensure the apples don't burn or stick to the pan.

Remove from the heat and transfer the cooked apples to a tray or bowl to cool.

Roll out the pastry on a lightly floured work surface to a large rectangle, 3-mm (⅛-in) thick. Cut out 7–8 circles of dough using a 15-cm (6-in) round pastry cutter or a saucer and a small sharp knife.

Line a large baking sheet with baking paper and place the pastry discs onto the lined sheet. Gently brush the edges of the pastry discs with water – this will help to seal the turnovers when it comes to folding them. Place 2 generous tablespoons of the filling mixture in the middle of each pastry disc. Carefully fold the disc over to form a half moon or small pasty shape and press the edges together to seal in the filling. Either use the teeth of a fork to press around the edge or carefully crimp the edges of the pastry between your thumb and forefinger. Insert the tip of a sharp knife into the middle of each turnover to allow the steam to escape as they bake.

Place the turnovers into the refrigerator to rest for at least 30 minutes.

Meanwhile, preheat the oven to 180°C fan (400°F/gas 6).

Generously glaze the turnovers with the beaten egg and sprinkle with plenty of Demerara sugar.

Bake for 15–18 minutes until golden all over and the bases are golden and flaky.

Tarte Tatin

This is not the easiest of desserts to master. One of the really important stages is cooking the apples in the caramel and reducing the liquid before adding the pastry. The reason for this is so that when we turn out the finished tart it is fully caramelised and not watery. Comice or Williams pears are a great alternative to apples.

250 g (9 oz/generous 1 cup) caster (superfine) sugar
125 g (4 oz) unsalted butter
6 Granny Smith apples
300 g (10½ oz) Puff Pastry (see pages 134–137)
plain (all-purpose) flour, for dusting

Add the sugar and butter to a 24-cm (9½-in) ovenproof frying pan (skillet) set over a medium-high heat. Melt the butter and sugar until it caramelises and turns a rich hazelnut colour.

Remove from the heat and allow the caramel to cool for 10–15 minutes while you prepare the apples. Peel and core the apples, then cut into quarters – you should have 24 pieces.

Arrange the apples in the frying pan starting from the edge and placing the quarters, cut-sides down, in a circular pattern on top of the caramel.

Cook for 20 minutes over a medium heat to caramelise the apples.

Remove from the heat and allow to cool for 15 minutes.

Meanwhile, preheat the oven to 170°C fan (375°F/gas 5).

Roll out the pastry on a lightly floured surface to a circle about 30 cm (12 in) in diameter. Remember to turn the pastry and dust with flour as you roll it to ensure it doesn't stick.

Carefully lay the puff pastry over the saucepan and push the excess pastry inside the edges of the pan. The trick is to tuck the excess pastry under the sides of the apples to form the pastry nest that will hold it together when it is turned out.

Transfer the pan to the oven and bake for 50 minutes–1 hour until the bubbling around the edges looks thick and syrupy, not watery.

Remove from the oven and allow to cool for 2–3 minutes only and then very carefully, but swiftly, turn it over onto a plate (it's safest with a seperate cloth in each hand!).

Serve hot from the oven with thick cream.

2 hours
Serves 6-8

Preparation - 15 minutes
Cooking - 25 minutes
Cooling - 15 minutes
Baking - 50 minutes-1 hour

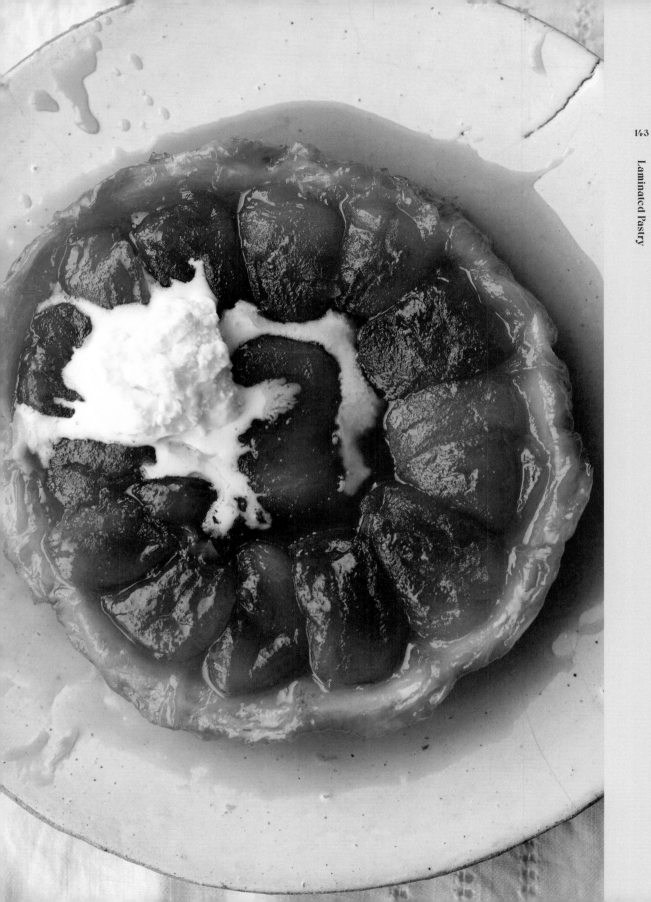

Millefeuille

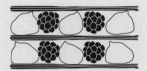

Millefeuille, or custard slice as we call it in the UK, is a wonderful thing. A key point to look out for is to make sure the pastry is completely baked through, so that it remains crisp when you add the pastry cream filling. Like many of our recipes, different fruits can be used to recreate this dessert, most soft fruits will be delicious. Some people like to top the millefeuille with a little icing sugar and blowtorch it, which can also be a really nice finish.

500 g (1 lb 2 oz) Puff Pastry
  (see pages 134–137)
plain (all-purpose) flour, for dusting

For the vanilla custard

1 vanilla pod
500 ml (2 cups) full-fat (whole) milk
6 egg yolks
125 g (4 oz/generous ½ cup) caster
  (superfine) sugar, plus extra
  as needed
40 g (1½ oz/generous ¼ cup) plain
  (all-purpose) flour

To finish

125 g (½ cup) double (heavy) cream
60 g (2 oz/¼ cup) caster (superfine)
  sugar
150 g (5 oz) raspberries (see also tip,
  overleaf)
icing (confectioner's) sugar,
  for dusting

Preheat the oven to 190ºC fan (400ºF/gas 6). Line a large baking sheet with baking paper.

Roll out the puff pastry on a lightly floured work surface into a rectangle about 24 x 36 cm (10 x 15 in) and 2-mm (¹⁄₁₆-in) thick.

Transfer the pastry to the prepared baking sheet. Prick the whole surface of the pastry with a fork all over. It's important to dock the whole surface of the pastry in this way.

Bake the pastry for 25 minutes until golden. Remove from the oven and leave to cool on a wire rack.

Meanwhile, prepare the custard. Split the vanilla pod open lengthways and scrape out the seeds. Put the seeds, pod and milk into a heavy-based saucepan and slowly bring to the boil, to infuse the vanilla.

Place the egg yolks and sugar in a bowl and mix together for a few seconds, then sift in the flour and mix together.

Pour the boiling milk over the yolk mixture, whisking constantly to prevent curdling, then return the mixture to the pan and cook over a medium heat, whisking constantly for about 3 minutes, until nice and thick.

Pass the custard through a fine sieve (strainer), then place a sheet of clingfilm (plastic wrap) on the surface of the custard or a light sprinkling of caster sugar to prevent a skin forming. Leave to cool, then chill in the refrigerator.

When the pastry has cooled, slice it in half through the middle so that you have two large thin rectangles. Cut each half into six evenly sized rectangles (about 6 x 12 cm/2½ x 5 in), so you have 12 rectangles in total.

Continued next page →

2 hours
Makes 4 double-layer
or 6 single-layer pastries

Preparation – 15 minutes
Baking – 25-30 minutes
Cooling – 1 hour
Assembly – 15 minutes

Whip the cream and sugar together until thick. Remove the chilled custard from the refrigerator and whisk to remove any lumps. Fold the whipped cream into the chilled custard and fill a piping bag with the mixture (it's important that the custard has cooled completely before mixing with the cream). Cut the end off the piping bag.

To assemble, take one sheet of pastry and pipe a small circle of cream (about 2 cm/¾ in) in one corner of the rectangle. Place a raspberry next to it. Continue alternately piping cream and adding raspberries until the pastry is covered. Place a second rectangle of pastry on top and generously dust this top layer with icing sugar.

You can continue to create a second tier in the same way for a classic millefeuille, if wished, or leave it as a single-layer pastry. Continue until you have used up all the cream, raspberries and pastry and ensure you finish the top layer of pastry with a generous dusting of icing sugar.

Tips

The custard filling will keep, covered, in the refrigerator for up to 5 days. The key is to cool the custard very quickly after cooking it. Use seasonal fruit as an alternative filling – blueberries and strawberries are very good, too.

ANATOMY OF MILLEFEUILLE

clean, square edges

visible open layers

fully crisped puff pastry

fresh, seasonal berries

Chocolate Pithiviers

This was the signature dessert of Bibendum restaurant back in the day. I worked here as a pastry chef in 1992 and it was my introduction to the cooking scene of London in the nineties. The kitchen was electric. One of my first jobs was to make the chocolate *pithiviers* and I'm going to share this with you now. In my mind, this is an infinitely better dessert than its successor, the chocolate fondant. The reason it is so special is that it has a melting gooey centre that is wrapped up in buttery flaky pastry. This combination of flavours is like nothing I've ever eaten in my life. It has to be cooked to order and eaten right away with lashings of extra-thick Jersey cream.

600 g (1 lb 5 oz) Puff Pastry
 (see pages 134–137)
plain (all-purpose) flour, for dusting
1 egg, beaten
icing (confectioner's) sugar,
 for dusting

For the filling

400 g (14 oz) Frangipane
 (see page 111)
100 g (3½ oz) Crème Pâtissière
 (see page 182)
50 g (2 oz) dark chocolate
 (70% cocoa solids), melted
50 g (2 oz/¼ cup) chocolate chips

Stage 1

To make the filling, add the frangipane, crème pâtissière, melted chocolate and chocolate chips to a large mixing bowl. Mix together until you have a smooth, well-combined mixture. Alternatively, mix in a stand mixer on slow speed for 2 minutes.

Cover the bowl and chill in the refrigerator for 2 hours or in the freezer for 30 minutes.

Stage 2

Divide the cooled filling mixture into four balls, each weighing 150 g (5 oz) or press the mixture into a single large disc about 20 cm (8 in) in diameter.

Roll out the pastry on a lightly floured work surface into a large circle, 4 mm (¼ in) thick. Remember to turn the pastry and dust with flour as you roll it to ensure it doesn't stick.

If making the individual *pithiviers,* cut out four discs using a 10-cm (4-in) round pastry cutter, then cut out four larger discs with a 12-cm (5-in) round cutter.

If making one large pithivier, cut out two discs, using 26-cm (10-in) and 30-cm (12-in) cake tins (pans) as guides to cut around.

Continued next page →

3½–6 hours
Makes 1 large or 4 small

Stage 1
Preparation – 5 minutes
Chilling – 30 minutes–2 hours

Stage 2
Preparation – 15 minutes
Chilling – 2–3 hours
Baking – 25–30 minutes

ANATOMY OF PITHIVIER

crisp pastry shell

open-layered,
flaky pastry

gooey chocolate
middle

fully cooked base

Continued →

Place the chocolate filling into the middle of the smaller disc/s and gently flatten the filling very slightly. Place the larger disc/s over the top and carefully tuck the top layer around the base, creating a clean seal all the way around. [photo 1 on page 152] Place onto a lined baking sheet, then cover and chill in the refrigerator for 2–3 hours.

Stage 3

When ready to bake, preheat the oven to 180°C fan (400°F/gas 6).

Generously glaze the pastry/pastries with beaten egg and dust with plenty of icing sugar. [photos 2 and 3 on page 152]

Bake for 25–30 minutes until the pastry is golden. The middle of each *pithivier* should still be a little runny.

Serve with extra-thick Jersey cream – this is a very decadent dessert!

Fruit Pithivier

For the filling

fruit compote of choice (see page 274 for our Cherry Compote)
400 g (14 oz) Frangipane (see page 111)

Follow the recipe from Stage 2 on the previous page, rolling out the puff pastry and cutting the discs as desired.

Spread a layer of fruit compote over the base disc, then pipe a generous layer of frangipane over the compote. Seal in the compote and frangipane with the top layer of pastry as described and chill for 2–3 hours.

Glaze and bake in the same way.

Lentil Rolls

This is a very satisfying alternative to a traditional sausage roll. Feel free to add plenty of seasonal herbs and spices to the lentil mix and put your own spin on it – curried spices work very nicely. Make sure you make the lentil mix well in advance so it is completely cool. These can also be made up and frozen to bake when you need them.

500 g (1 lb 2 oz) Puff Pastry
   (see pages 134–137)
plain (all-purpose) flour, for dusting
1 egg yolk, beaten
vegetable oil, for greasing
fennel seeds, for sprinkling

For the lentil filling

500 g (1 lb 2 oz/2½ cups) Puy lentils,
   rinsed
2 litres (8 cups) water
1 onion, finely chopped
2 garlic cloves, crushed
1 ripe plum tomato
100 g (3½ oz) flat-leaf parsley stalks
2 sprigs of fresh rosemary, leaves
   picked
6 strands fresh thyme
1 bay leaf

For the seasoning

1 onion, finely chopped
1 tablespoon onion powder
1 tablespoon garlic granules
1 teaspoon mustard powder
2 tablespoons chopped flat-leaf
   parsley
1 tablespoon chopped rosemary
1 tablespoon chopped thyme
sea salt and freshly ground black
   pepper, to taste

Stage 1

To prepare the filling, place the lentils in a large saucepan, cover with the measured water and add the remaining filling ingredients. Use a wooden spoon to squash the tomato into the lentils (this will soften the lentils when cooking). Bring to the boil, then reduce the heat and simmer for 30 minutes or until the lentils are soft.

Strain the lentils, discarding the bay leaf, thyme and parsley stalks.

While the lentils are still warm, place half of them into a blender or food processor and blitz to a smooth purée.

Add the lentil purée to the remaining cooked lentils in a large mixing bowl, along with all of the seasoning ingredients. Fold together (you may find it easier to do this by hand). Taste and adjust the seasoning. Cover and refrigerate for at least 6 hours or overnight to develop the flavours.

Stage 2

On a lightly floured work surface, roll out the pastry to a 45 x 32-cm (18 x 13-in) rectangle. Cut in half lengthways. Lay the rectangles of pastry side by side and spread the filling in an even line along the length of each rectangle, shaping it into a sausage shape and leaving a 3-cm (1-in) gap around the edges. Brush the edges of the pastry with egg yolk, then fold one side of the pastry over to meet the other side and enclose the filling. Press down around the edges, then use the teeth of a fork dipped in flour to press along the seams and seal the joins. Place the rolls back into the refrigerator for 2 hours to firm up.

Meanwhile, preheat the oven to 180°C fan (400°F/gas 6). Line a baking sheet with baking paper and lightly oil it.

Brush the rolls with more egg yolk and sprinkle with fennel seeds, then cut each roll into four smaller rolls, each about 8-cm (3-in) long.

Place the rolls onto the lined baking sheet, leaving a bit of space between them. Bake for 30–35 minutes until crispy golden brown and hot throughout.

9½ hours (or 2 days)
Makes 8

Stage 1

Preparation – 45 minutes
Chilling – 6 hours or overnight

Stage 2

Preparation – 15 minutes
Chilling – 2 hours
Baking – 30–35 minutes

Plain Croissants

It's been five years since we wrote the last cookbook, but the process for our croissants remains the same. A classic recipe just needs time and practice. We've taken our croissant dough a little bit further in this book, playing with flavours for something deeply satisfying – our Babka Buns on page 162 really take the dough to new heights.

For the pre-ferment

500 g (1 lb 2 oz/3½ cups) strong white (bread) flour
12 g (2 teaspoons) fine sea salt
55 g (2 oz/¼ cup) caster (superfine) sugar
40 g unsalted butter, softened
30 g (2 tablespoons) fresh yeast
140 g (generous ½ cup) cold water
140 g (generous ½ cup) full-fat (whole) milk

To finish

250 g (9 oz) cold unsalted butter
extra flour, for dusting
1 egg, beaten

Day 1

To make the pre-ferment, combine the flour, salt and sugar in a bowl. Add the butter and crumb through with your fingers.

In a separate bowl, add the yeast to the water and milk, then mix until dissolved.

Make a well in the middle of the flour mixture, pour in the liquid and mix together until all of the ingredients are incorporated (try not to overwork the dough). Push down so the dough is spread out in the bottom of the bowl, then cover and refrigerate for 8–12 hours or overnight.

Day 2

An hour before you take the dough from the refrigerator, use a rolling pin to gently pound the butter between two pieces of baking paper to make it square and flat, about 5-mm (¼-in) thick. Place the butter back into the refrigerator for 40 minutes (it's important that the dough and butter are the same temperature). [See photos 1 and 2 on page 135]

Place the chilled dough onto a lightly floured work surface and roll it out to a 25-cm (10-in) square. Turn the dough so it looks like a diamond, then roll each corner out so you have a cross shape with four thin flaps and a slightly raised square of dough in the middle. [Photo 3, page 135]

Place the butter in the middle of the dough, then start to encase it. Fold the top and bottom flaps over to enclose the dough, pulling them slightly so they cover it as much as possible. Then pull the side flaps over, so the butter is fully enclosed as if in an envelope. Tap the dough gently with the side of the rolling pin to help seal it. [Photos 4, 5 and 6, page 135]

With the seam running top to bottom, roll the dough out into a long rectangular shape, about 25-cm (10-in) wide and 70-cm (27-in) long.

Continued next page →

3 days
Makes 12

Day 1
Preparation – 10 minutes
Chilling – 8–12 hours or
overnight

Day 2
Preparation – 15 minutes +
2 stages of 5 minutes each
Chilling – 14 hours or overnight

Preparation – 20 minutes
Proving – 2 hours
Baking – 12–15 minutes

157

Laminated Pastry

Brush off any flour and fold the dough in thirds (this is called a half fold). Gently tap the dough with the rolling pin, then place back into the refrigerator to rest for 1 hour. [Photos 7 and 8, page 137]

Take the dough out of the refrigerator and place onto a lightly floured surface once again. With the seam running top to bottom, roll the dough out into a long rectangular shape, about 25-cm (10-in) wide and 70-cm (27-in) long. [Photos 9 and 10, page 137]

Brush off any flour and give the dough another half fold. Gently tap the dough with the rolling pin then place back into the fridge to rest for another hour. [Photo 11, page 137]

Repeat one more time so your croissant dough has had a total of three half folds. Cover and refrigerate for at least 12 hours (this will help hold the layers you have created and make rolling out easier in the final stage). [Photo 12, page 137]

Day 3

Take the dough out of the refrigerator and place onto a lightly floured surface. With the seam running side to side, roll the dough out so it is about 25-cm (10-in) long. Turn the dough so the seam is running top to bottom and roll the dough out to about 70-cm (27-in) long. The final measurement should be 25 x 70 cm (10 x 27 in) and the dough should be about 4-mm (¼-in) thick.

Turn the dough so the longest edge is facing you and use a sharp knife to cut the dough into 12 equal triangles. The base of each triangle should be roughly four fingers wide.

Cut a small slit about 5-mm (¼-in) long at the base of each triangle. Gently stretch your triangle out, then roll up your croissant making sure the tail is tucked under the rolled-up croissant.

Place the croissants on a baking sheet lined with baking paper, ensuring they are evenly spaced out. Brush each croissant with beaten egg and leave to prove in a warmish place (ideally about 24°C/75°F) for about 2 hours. During this time they should double in size and you will be able to see the layers you have created. When they're ready to bake, they should also have a nice wobble to them. If they are not ready after 2 hours, give them a bit longer – they will be worth the wait!

Preheat the oven to 190°C fan (400°F/gas 6). Place the baking sheet in the oven and lightly spritz the oven chamber with a water spray.

Bake for 12–15 minutes until the croissants are a nice golden colour and slightly crispy on the outside. Take out and enjoy.

Pain au Praline

Traditionally, French bakers use day-old croissants or pain au chocolat to make these pastries. They are filled, then re-baked in the oven a second time. The frangipane filling gives a fabulously moist inside while the outside remains crispy and fresh. The pistachio version is very similar, we just use some roasted pistachio paste in place of hazelnuts and some chopped pistachios on top. These really are quite sensational.

6 day-old pain au chocolat (bought)
300 g (10½ oz) Frangipane
   (see page 111)
icing (confectioner's) sugar,
   for dusting

For the praline crumb

70 g (2½ oz/½ cup) toasted
   hazelnuts
70 g (2½ oz/scant ⅓ cup) caster
   (superfine) sugar

For the syrup

50 g (2 oz/¼ cup) caster
   (superfine) sugar
100 g (scant ½ cup) water

To make the praline crumb, line a baking sheet with baking paper and spread the hazelnuts over it.

Melt the sugar in a saucepan over a medium-high heat until it reaches a dark brown caramel colour, then remove from the heat and pour over the hazelnuts. Leave to cool for 2 hours or until completely solid.

Break up the praline with a rolling pin and add the shards to a food processor. Blitz for 3 minutes to a rough breadcrumb texture.

To prepare the syrup, add the sugar and water to a saucepan set over a medium-high heat, bring to the boil, then reduce the heat and simmer for 5 minutes or until all of the sugar has dissolved and the liquid has reduced by about a third. Remove from the heat.

Preheat the oven to 160°C fan (350°F/gas 4). Line a large baking sheet with baking paper.

Stir 100 g (3½ oz) of the praline crumb into the frangipane.

Slice each pain au chocolat horizontally through the middle. Dip each half of the pain au chocolat in the syrup and place onto the lined baking sheet. Spoon 50–60 g (2 oz) of the frangipane onto the base of each pain au chocolat and place the tops back on. Spread a little of the remaining frangipane on top of each pastry and sprinkle the remaining praline crumb on top.

Bake for 30 minutes.

Remove from the oven and allow to cool briefly. Finish with a dusting of icing sugar.

For a pistachio version

Follow the instructions above, adding 100 g (3½ oz/⅓ cup) of pistachio paste to your frangipane in place of the praline crumb.

Before baking, spread a little pistachio frangipane on the top of the pain au chocolat and sprinkle with some chopped pistachio nuts.

Bake for 25 minutes as above.

2 hours 50 minutes
Makes 6

Preparation – 5 minutes
Cooling – 2 hours

Preparation – 15 minutes
Baking – 25–30 minutes

Babka Buns

These are a recent addition to the Bread Ahead family and are quite different to the Babka Loaf. We use laminated croissant pastry dough, although the chocolate filling is the same. We find the buttery croissant pastry gives the most amazing flavour when baked. We top them with a little egg wash and pearl sugar, which helps to give them a nice crunch on top. It's important not to overbake them as they need to remain quite moist and juicy inside.

800 g (1 lb 12 oz) Croissant Pastry
   (see pages 156–158)

For the filling

55 g (2 oz) unsalted butter
30 g (1 oz/¼ cup) cocoa powder
55 g (2 oz) dark chocolate, chopped
1 large egg
55 g (2 oz/¼ cup) caster (superfine)
   sugar

To finish

1 egg, beaten
sugar nibs, for sprinkling

Roll out the croissant dough to a rectangle the size of a conventional baking sheet (45 x 50 cm/18 x 20 in) and about 3-mm (⅛-in) thick.

To make the filling, melt the butter and cocoa powder together in a small saucepan and stir to combine. While the mixture is still warm, add the chopped chocolate and stir until the chocolate has completely melted into the butter.

In a separate bowl, whisk together the egg and sugar until the sugar has started to break down. Add the egg and sugar mixture to the chocolate mixture and whisk until completely combined.

Use a palette knife to spread the filling mixture over the rectangle of croissant dough. Leave a small strip clear of any filling along one of the long edges, then brush this strip with a little water (this strip will be used to seal the dough once it's rolled). Roll up the dough lengthways, gently pressing the filling-free edge into the dough to seal it. Rest the dough seam-side down for a moment.

Cut the roll into 12 pieces, each about 4-cm (1½-in) thick. Place each round into the individual holes of a 12-hole silicone mould or muffin tin (pan) and leave to prove at room temperature for 1 hour.

Meanwhile, preheat the oven to 180°C fan (400°F/gas 6).

Brush the proved buns with the beaten egg and sprinkle with sugar nibs. Bake for 15 minutes, then turn the pan around in the oven and bake for a further 10 minutes until golden brown.

1 hour 40 minutes (+ 2 days to
make the croissant dough)
Makes 12

Preparation – 15 minutes
Proving – 1 hour
Baking – 25 minutes

ANATOMY OF A BABKA BUN

moist texture

visible, flaky, open layers

golden crisp outer

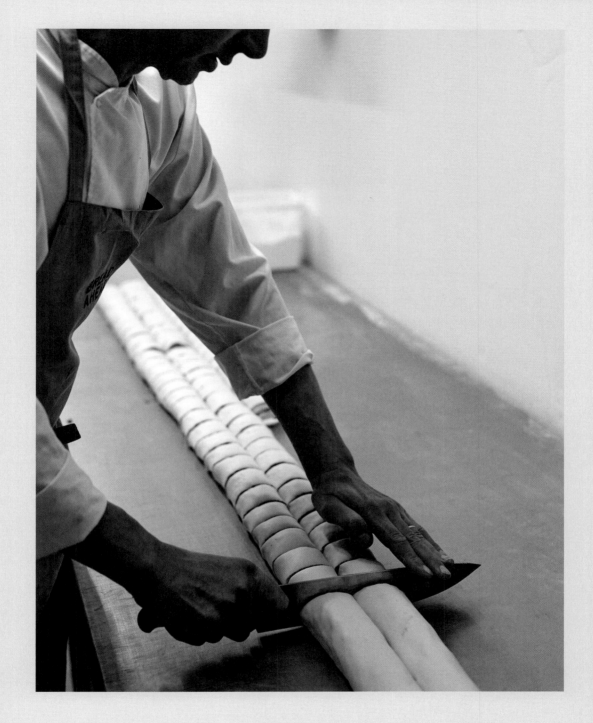

Saffron Buns

Saffron buns are one of the key bakes in our Scandinavian baking course. Saffron is such a special flavour that seems to work particularly well with a buttery, layered pastry. They're quite different to a classic Scandinavian saffron bun, but I think you will find these pretty remarkable.

pinch of saffron threads
140 g (generous ½ cup) freshly boiled water
500 g (1 lb 2 oz/3½ cups) strong white (bread) flour, plus extra for dusting
12 g (2 teaspoons) fine sea salt
55 g (2 oz/¼ cup) caster (superfine) sugar
40 g (1½ oz) unsalted butter, softened
30 g (2 tablespoons) fresh yeast or 15 g (5 teaspoons) dried active yeast
140 g full-fat (whole) milk

To finish

250 g (9 oz) cold unsalted butter, plus extra for greasing (optional)
50 g (2 oz/¼ cup) soft light brown sugar
1 egg, beaten
sugar nibs (optional)
flaked (slivered) almonds (optional)

Day 1

Infuse the saffron in the freshly boiled water and leave to cool.

Place the flour, salt and sugar in a bowl and combine. Add the butter and rub in with your fingertips to fine crumbs.

Add the yeast and milk to the cooled saffron water, then mix until the yeast is dissolved.

Make a well in the middle of the dry mixture and pour in the liquid. Mix together until all of the dry ingredients are incorporated (try not to overwork the dough). Knead very briefly in the bowl until a smooth dough is formed. Push down so the dough is spread out in the bottom of the bowl, then cover and chill in the refrigerator for 8–12 hours.

Day 2

Pound the cold butter with a rolling pin to make it nice and flat and remove the dough from the refrigerator. Proceed to laminate the dough with the butter, according to the method on pages 156–158.

Take the chilled laminated saffron dough out of the refrigerator and place on a lightly floured work surface. Turn the dough so the seam is running top to bottom and roll it out to about 80-cm (31-in) long, 40-cm (16-in) wide and about 4-mm (¼-in) thick.

Give the dough a quarter turn so that you have the long edge of the large rectangle facing you, then roll it up lengthways into a tight roll. With the seam of the roll on the bottom, use a sharp knife to cut the roll into 12 even rounds, each about 70 g (2½ oz).

Continued next page →

2 days
Makes 12

Day 1
Preparation – 15 minutes
Resting – 8-12 hours

Day 2
Lamination stage – 3 hours
Preparation – 20 minutes
Proving – 2 hours (or up to 12 hours in the refrigerator)
Baking – 12-15 minutes

ANATOMY OF SAFFRON BUNS

flaky outer crust

bright golden
yellow

open, airy
texture inside

Continued →

Sprinkle most of the soft brown sugar into the holes of a muffin tin, reserving about 1 tablespoon of sugar to sprinkle on top before baking. You can use any size or shape of tin that you have available. If you're using a metal muffin tin, you will need to grease it with a little butter first. We use silicone moulds that don't need greasing.

Place the dough rounds into each sugared hole of the muffin tin and leave to rise in a warmish place (ideally 24°C/75°F) for about 2 hours. You could also prove slowly in the refrigerator for up to 12 hours. When they're ready to bake, they should have a nice wobble to them. If they are not ready after 2 hours, give them a bit longer – it will be worth the wait!

Preheat the oven to 190°C fan (400°F/gas 6).

Brush each bun with egg wash and sprinkle the tops with the remaining soft brown sugar. Place the tin in the oven and lightly spritz the oven chamber with a water spray or place a ¼ cup of water in a baking dish on the bottom of the oven. Bake for 12–15 minutes until the buns are a nice golden colour and slightly crispy on the outside.

Remove and enjoy.

Savoury Croissants

This is a perfect way to use up day-old croissants, so never throw them away. Start off by making the bechamel and allowing it to cool, then try any of these savoury variations. Do be generous with the fillings and don't skimp with the fresh herbs.

6 Plain Croissants (see page 156)
sea salt and freshly ground black pepper

For the béchamel sauce

250 ml (1 cup) full-fat (whole) milk
½ teaspoon English mustard
pinch of salt
50 g (2 oz) unsalted butter
30 g (1 oz/2 tablespoons) plain
(all-purpose) flour

For the spinach and goat's cheese filling

25 g (¾ oz) unsalted butter
150 g (5 oz) fresh spinach
150 g (5 oz) goat's cheese

For the herbed mushroom filling

25 g (¾ oz) unsalted butter
500 g (1 lb 2 oz) button mushrooms,
finely sliced
pinch of fine sea salt
handful of fresh herbs (tarragon,
parsley or dill), finely chopped
mature Cheddar cheese, to taste

For the roasted tomato and wild garlic filling

6 plum tomatoes, halved
2 tablespoons olive oil
dried herbs of choice, for sprinkling
small bunch of wild garlic, finely
chopped (or ½ garlic bulb, cut
through the middle horizontally)

To make the béchamel sauce, put the milk, mustard and salt into a saucepan set over a medium heat and bring the milk to a simmer.

In a separate saucepan, gently melt the butter. Once melted, add the flour and stir it in. Continue stirring the butter and flour mixture together over a medium heat until it forms a smooth paste.

Add the milk to the butter pan and stir together. Continue to cook the sauce until it thickens, stirring often so it doesn't catch on the bottom of the pan. Cover the surface of the sauce with clingfilm (plastic wrap) and leave to cool.

For the spinach and goat's cheese filling

Melt the butter in a large pan, add the spinach and cook until the spinach has completely wilted and absorbed the butter. Spread the cooked spinach over a tray to cool.

Roughly chop the goat's cheese and transfer to a large mixing bowl along with the cooled béchamel and spinach and stir to combine. Season to taste.

For the herbed mushroom filling

Melt the butter in a large frying pan (skillet) over a medium-high heat. Once the butter has melted and starts to foam, add the mushrooms and sauté them for several minutes until they start to brown. Add a pinch of salt to release some of the juices. Continue to cook the mushrooms until they have re-absorbed all of the cooking liquids, then transfer them to a tray and leave to cool completely.

Add the chopped herbs to a mixing bowl along with the cooled béchamel sauce and mushrooms. Grate in some cheese – feel free to use as much or as little as you like, we use about 2 tablespoons per croissant. Stir to combine, then taste and season as needed.

Continued next page →

1¼-2 hours (plus 3 days to make
the croissants from scratch)
Each filling recipe makes enough
to fill 6 croissants

Preparation – 20 minutes
Cooling – 30 minutes

Baking – 25 minutes
(+ 45-50 minutes if roasting
the tomatoes)

Continued →

For the roasted tomato and wild garlic filling

Preheat the oven to 140ºC fan (325ºF/gas 3). Line a baking sheet with baking paper.

Place the tomatoes, cut-sides up, on the baking sheet and drizzle with the olive oil and selection of dried herbs. If using a regular garlic bulb, add this to the baking tray too.

Bake for 45–50 minutes or until the tomatoes have softened and started to dry and the juices have caramelised slightly. Leave to cool.

If using chopped wild garlic, fold it through the cooled bechamel sauce. Alternatively, if using roasted garlic, squeeze the softened garlic flesh out of the skins, add to the bechamel and stir together. Season to taste.

To finish

Preheat the oven to 160ºC fan (350ºF/gas 4).

Carefully slice each croissant horizontally through the middle and fill with plenty of your chosen filling mixture. If making the roasted tomato and wild garlic croissants, fill with a few spoonfuls of garlic bechamel and top each with two tomato halves.

Place the croissants onto a lined baking sheet and bake for 25 minutes.

Tips

– Frozen spinach works really well, but fresh is best if you can get it. Leave the goat's cheese quite chunky so you get nice little nuggets of it through the croissant. If you don't have goat's cheese, any other hard cheeses, such as Cheddar, are also delicious.

– The tomato and wild garlic croissant is very much a seasonal classic on the Bread Ahead table, as wild garlic has a splendidly limited season. It's important to really dry out the tomatoes as you don't want them too watery. You could also use cherry tomatoes, which will lend a lovely sweetness.

Spinach and Feta Rolls

By using croissant pastry here, we achieve a delicious sweetness and buttery-ness in the finished bake. You could use puff pastry, but croissant is better. A little touch of nutmeg really does highlight the flavours of spinach. Fresh spinach is best, if using frozen make sure you drain it thoroughly.

plain (all-purpose) flour, for dusting
500 g (1 lb 2 oz) Croissant Pastry
   (see page 156)
1 egg, beaten

For the filling

30 g (1 oz) unsalted butter
500 g (1 lb 2 oz) fresh spinach
250 g (9 oz) feta cheese
nutmeg, for grating
sea salt and freshly ground
   black pepper

To prepare the filling, melt the butter in a large saucepan over a medium heat. When the butter begins to foam, add the spinach and cook until it has completely cooked down. Spread the spinach over a tray to cool down.

Put the cooled spinach into a mixing bowl, crumble in the feta and mix in, then season with salt and pepper and a fresh grating of nutmeg.

Fill a piping bag fitted with a large nozzle with the spinach mixture.

On a lightly floured work surface, roll out the croissant pastry to 5-mm (¼-in) thick and the size of a large baking sheet, about 40 x 50 cm (16 x 20 in). Slice into two large rectangles through the length of the pastry and lay them side by side.

Pipe the filling mixture in two long strips down the middle of each rectangle of pastry, as if making a sausage roll. Brush all the edges of the pastry with beaten egg or water, then fold one side of the pastry over to meet the other side to enclose the filling. Press the pastry down around the edges, then use the back of a fork dipped in flour to press down along the seam to seal the join.

Cover with a damp cloth and leave the pastry to prove for 1 hour.

Preheat the oven to 180°C fan (400°F/gas 6). Line 2 baking sheets with baking paper.

When proved, cut each pastry roll into 3–4 individual rolls and place them on the prepared baking sheets, spaced well apart.

Brush the top of the pastries with beaten egg and make a few small diagonal slashes in the top of each.

Bake for 18–20 minutes until golden and crisp. Ensure the bottom of each roll is cooked through and golden brown.

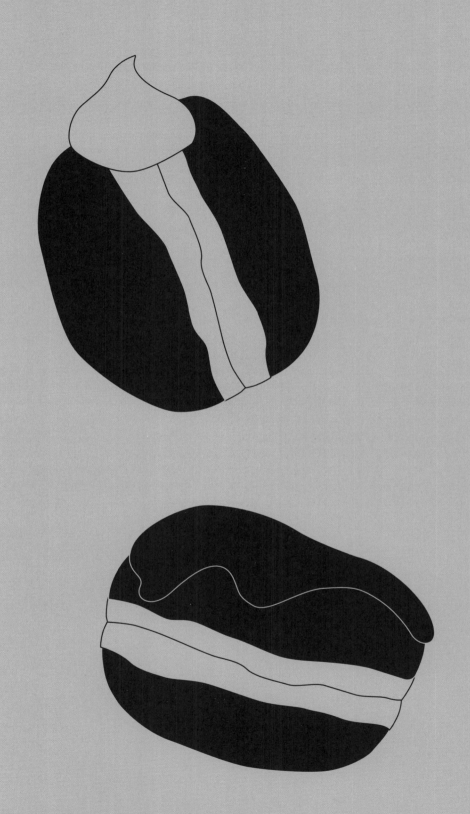

five

Doughnuts & Fillings

Plain Doughnuts

We've elaborated on flavours, but the base of our doughnuts will always remain the same. We started with five flavours for the first couple of years, but we've added a few new ones over time, and they're all absolutely delicious.

For the dough

250 g (9 oz/ 1¾ cups) strong white (bread) flour, plus extra for dusting (optional)
30 g (1 oz/3 tablespoons) caster (superfine) sugar
5 g (¾ teaspoons) fine sea salt
zest of ½ small lemon
75 g (scant 5 tablespoons) water
2 eggs
8 g (1½ teaspoons) fresh yeast or 4 g (1¼ teaspoons) dried active yeast
65 g (2¼ oz) unsalted butter, softened

To finish

2 litres (8 cups) oil (rapeseed/canola, sunflower or corn), for deep-frying, plus extra for greasing (optional)
200 g (7 oz/ ¾ cup) caster (superfine) sugar, for dusting

Day 1

Bring all of the dough ingredients, apart from the butter, together in a bowl. Turn the dough out onto the work surface and knead for 5 minutes using the heel of your hand. (If using a stand mixer, see Tip overleaf.)

Let the dough rest for 1 minute.

Start to add the butter a quarter at a time, kneading it in until it is all incorporated. Knead the dough for a further 5 minutes until it is glossy, smooth and very elastic when pulled.

Return the dough to the bowl, cover with a plate and leave to prove until doubled in size, about 1½ hours.

Knock back the dough, re-cover the bowl and refrigerate overnight.

Day 2

Remove the dough from the refrigerator and cut into 10 pieces, about 50 g (2 oz) each. Dust a large baking sheet with flour or grease with a little oil.

Roll the dough into 10 smooth, tight buns using the method on page 38 and place them on the prepared baking sheet, leaving plenty of room between them as you don't want them to stick together while they prove. Cover lightly with a damp dish towel or lightly oiled cling film (plastic wrap) and leave to prove for about 2 hours, or until doubled in size.

Get your deep-fat fryer ready or fill a heavy-based saucepan up to the halfway point with oil (be extremely careful – hot oil is very dangerous). Heat the oil to 180ºC (350°F). The gauge on the fryer or a kitchen thermometer really is essential here for accuracy.

Continued next page →

2 days
Makes 10

Day 1
Preparation - 15 minutes
Proving - 1½ hours
Resting - overnight

Day 2
Preparation - 10 minutes
Proving - 2 hours
Frying - 15-20 minutes

ANATOMY OF DOUGHNUTS

golden, sugared
outer crust

even buttery
crumb

the 'band of truth' shows
consistent, even proving

Continued →

When the oil is heated to the correct temperature, carefully remove the doughnuts from the tray by sliding a floured dough scraper or spatula underneath them, taking care not to deflate them, and carefully lower them into the oil. Do not overcrowd the fryer – cook 2–3 at a time, depending on the size of your pan. Fry for 2 minutes on each side until golden brown – they will puff up and float.

Remove from the fryer with a slotted spoon and place on paper towels to drain, then toss the doughnuts in the caster sugar while still warm.

Repeat until all doughnuts are fried BUT make sure the oil temperature is correct each time before frying – if it is too high, they will colour too quickly and burn, and will be raw in the middle; if it is too low, the doughnuts will absorb the oil and become greasy.

Let cool before filling.

To fill the doughnuts, make a hole in the crease of each one with a butter knife (anywhere in the white line between the fried top and bottom). Fill a piping bag with your desired filling and pipe it into the doughnut until plump.

The doughnuts are best eaten immediately.

Tip

If using a stand mixer, bring all of the dough ingredients, apart from the butter, together using a dough hook, and mix for a few minutes on medium speed. Let the dough rest for 1 minute. Take care that the mixer doesn't overheat – it needs to rest as well as the dough! Start it up again on a medium speed and slowly add the butter to the dough – about a quarter at a time. Once it is all incorporated, mix on high speed for 5 minutes.

Vanilla Custard Doughnuts

The classic vanilla doughnut is by far the most popular. There is something so simple yet so delicious about vanilla custard, also known as crème pâtissière, it's hard to put your finger on. I think it's the indulgent texture and the simplicity of the flavours that just work so well.

10 Plain Doughnuts
  (see pages 178–181)

For the crème pâtissière (vanilla custard)

½ vanilla pod
250 g (1 cup) full-fat (whole) milk
3 egg yolks
60 g (2 oz/⅓ cup) caster (superfine) sugar
30 g (1 oz/3 heaped tablespoons) plain (all-purpose) flour

To finish

60 g (¼ cup) double (heavy) cream
30 g (1 oz/2 tablespoons) caster (superfine) sugar

Split the vanilla pod open lengthways and scrape out the seeds. Put the seeds, pod and milk into a heavy-based saucepan and bring slowly to the boil, to infuse the vanilla.

Meanwhile, place the egg yolks and sugar in a bowl and mix together for a few seconds, then sift in the flour and mix together. Pour the boiling milk over the yolk mixture, whisking constantly to prevent curdling, then return the mixture to the pan and cook over a medium heat, whisking constantly for about 3 minutes until nice and thick.

Pass through a fine sieve (strainer), then place a sheet of baking paper or a scattering of caster sugar on the surface of the custard to prevent a skin forming (don't forget to keep your vanilla pod – wash and dry it to use again). Leave the custard to cool, then refrigerate until cold.

To finish, whip the cream and sugar together until thick, then fold in the chilled custard until well combined. Transfer to a piping bag and you're ready to fill your doughnuts (see page 181)!

1 hour 20 minutes
Makes enough to fill
10 doughnuts

Preparation – 15 minutes
Cooling – 1 hour
Finishing – 5 minutes

Eton Mess Doughnuts

We start making these at the beginning of Wimbledon week each year, which we see as the official start of summer. British strawberries, Chantilly cream, meringue and crème pâtissière are folded together to recreate this classic dessert encased in a doughnut. Game, set and match.

10 Plain Doughnuts
  (see pages 178–181)

For the meringue

2 egg whites
125 g (4 oz/generous ½ cup) caster (superfine) sugar

For the crème pâtissière

½ vanilla pod
250 g (1 cup) full-fat (whole) milk
3 egg yolks
60 g (2 oz/⅓ cup) caster (superfine) sugar
30 g (1 oz/3 heaped tablespoons) plain (all-purpose) flour

To finish

1 punnet of strawberries
60 g (¼ cup) double (heavy) cream
1 tablespoon caster (superfine) sugar

Preheat the oven to 110°C (90°C fan/gas ¼). Line a baking sheet with baking paper.

In a mixing bowl, whisk the egg whites until frothy and turning white in colour. Add the sugar and continue to whisk until stiff peaks form. (You can do this in a stand mixer or with an electric whisk if you wish.)

Fill a piping bag fitted with a 15-mm (¾-in) plain nozzle (or cut a hole in the end of the bag) with the meringue mixture. Pipe pencils of meringue, each about 8-cm (3-in) long, onto the prepared baking sheet.

Bake for 2 hours. You do not want the meringue to colour, so a low and slow bake is essential.

Meanwhile, prepare the crème pâtissière according to the method on page 182.

To finish, chop the strawberries into 1-cm (½-in) pieces (reserving a few to slice and decorate the doughnuts) and roughly crush about half of the meringues. Whip the cream and sugar together until thick, then fold in the chilled custard. Finally, fold through the chopped strawberries and crushed meringues. Fill a piping bag with the mixture.

Fill each doughnut with the cream mixture (see page 181), top with a generous shard of meringue and a sliced strawberry.

2½ hours
Makes enough to fill
10 doughnuts

Preparation – 15 minutes
Baking – 2 hours
Finishing – 15 minutes

Tip

These doughnuts look beautiful when finished with a little drizzle of strawberry coulis. If you have some strawberries spare, you can make the coulis by pressing chopped strawberries through a fine mesh sieve (strainer) with the back of a wooden spoon. Alternatively, you can pulse them in a blender, then sieve to remove the seeds.

Lemon Curd Doughnuts

When I was young, lemon curd came in a jam jar and didn't taste of lemon. I have created a version that is worthy of the name lemon curd. Let's face it, you want to feel like you're biting into a lemon. The important part of this process is to cook it slowly, then allow it to fully cool overnight in the refrigerator. The acidity of the lemon works really well in a doughnut. We like to finish it with a little bit of grated lime zest.

10 Plain Doughnuts
(see pages 178–181)

For the lemon curd

125 g (4 oz) unsalted butter
20 g (¾ oz/2 heaped tablespoons)
plain (all-purpose) flour
125 g (½ cup) lemon juice (or half
and half lemon and lime juice)
125 g (4 oz/ ½ cup) caster (superfine)
sugar
2 eggs, plus 3 egg yolks

Optional

60 g (¼ cup) double (heavy) cream
grated zest of ½ lime

Put the butter and flour into a heavy-based saucepan set over a medium heat and cook until the butter has melted, whisking well to combine.

In a separate saucepan, combine the lemon juice and sugar and bring to the boil, stirring occasionally to ensure the sugar has dissolved.

Carefully pour the boiling lemon mixture into the butter and flour, whisking as you go. Bring to the boil and simmer for 1 minute.

Remove from the heat and add the eggs and yolks, whisking until well combined. Return to a low heat and cook the curd for 1 minute, stirring as it thickens.

Pour the cooked curd into a tray or large bowl to cool it. It will keep for several weeks in a sealed jar/container in the refrigerator.

At this point, you can fill the doughnuts with the pure curd, or you can fold in a little whipped cream to make them lighter (I always find this quite amusing as there is nothing 'light' about whipped cream!).

If using, whisk the cream until thickened to stiff peaks, then fold through the lemon curd.

Transfer the filling to a piping bag and get ready to fill some doughnuts.

Pipe each doughnut with about 50–60 g (2 oz) of filling for a really satisfying experience (see page 181). We love to finish these with a little grated lime zest for an extra zingy finish.

50 minutes
Makes enough to fill
10 doughnuts

Preparation – 15 minutes
Cooling – 30 minutes
Finishing – 5 minutes

Pumpkin Special Doughnuts

We developed these doughnuts for Halloween. Taste-wise, they're a bit like a crème brûlée doughnut – pretty sensational. They are a lot of work though, so we only do them on one day each year!

10 Plain Doughnuts
(see pages 178–181)

For the pumpkin purée

1 small squash/pumpkin

For the crème pâtissière

½ vanilla pod
250 g (1 cup) full-fat (whole) milk
3 egg yolks
60 g (2 oz/⅓ cup) caster (superfine) sugar
30 g (1 oz/3 heaped tablespoons) plain (all-purpose) flour

For the cream filling

60 g (¼ cup) double (heavy) cream

For the toffee topping

250 g (9 oz/generous 1 cup) caster (superfine) sugar
50 g (2 oz) unsalted butter

Start by making the pumpkin purée. Preheat the oven to 150°C fan (350°F/gas 4).

Slice your pumpkin in half and remove and discard the seeds and stringy flesh. Chop each half into quarters, carefully remove the skin with a vegetable peeler, then chop into 1-cm (½-in) cubes. Place the pumpkin cubes onto a baking sheet and bake for 1 hour until the pumpkin is quite dry and lightly golden.

Transfer the pumpkin to a food processor and pulse to a purée. Leave to cool.

Meanwhile, prepare the crème pâtissière. Split the vanilla pod lengthways and scrape out the seeds. Put the seeds, pod and milk into a heavy-based saucepan and bring slowly to the boil, to infuse the vanilla.

Meanwhile, place the egg yolks and sugar in a bowl and mix together for a few seconds, then sift in the flour and mix together. Pour the boiling milk over the yolk mixture, whisking constantly to prevent curdling, then return the mixture to the pan and cook over a medium heat, whisking constantly for about 3 minutes until nice and thick.

Pass through a fine sieve (strainer), then place a sheet of baking paper or a scattering of caster sugar on the surface of the crème pâtissière to prevent a skin forming (don't forget to keep your vanilla pod – wash and dry it to use again). Leave to cool, then refrigerate until cold.

Whip the double cream in a large mixing bowl until thickened to stiff peaks.

Measure out 200 g (7 oz) of the cooled pumpkin purée. Add the crème pâtissière and pumpkin purée to the whipped cream and gently fold together until the mixture is smooth and well combined. Fill a piping bag with the pumpkin custard.

2½ hours
Makes enough to fill
10 doughnuts

Preparation – 15 minutes
Baking – 1 hour
Cooling – 1 hour
Finishing – 15 minutes

Pipe a generous amount of custard into each doughnut (see page 181). We recommend at least 60 g (2 oz) per doughnut for a really satisfying experience.

Finally, prepare the toffee topping. Put the sugar and butter into a heavy-based saucepan set over a medium heat. Heat for several minutes until the sugar has melted and the mixture has the consistency of thick honey and has turned a rich caramel colour.

Remove the pan from the heat and very carefully dip one half of each filled doughnut into the caramel. Leave to set before devouring.

Pistachio Custard Doughnuts

Roasted pistachio paste is a specialist ingredient, but worth taking the time to find. There are plenty of online stockists selling high-quality pistachio paste. For me, the pistachio doughnut has been one of the highlights of the celebrated Bread Ahead doughnut range. It has a perfect combination of nutty savouriness and sweetness, which complements the fluffy doughnut shell.

10 Plain Doughnuts
  (see pages 178–181)

For the pistachio custard

½ vanilla pod
250 g (1 cup) full-fat (whole) milk
3 egg yolks
60 g (2 oz/⅓ cup) caster (superfine)
  sugar
30 g (1 oz/3 heaped tablespoons)
  plain (all-purpose) flour
30 g (1 oz/2 tablespoons) roasted
  pistachio paste

To finish

60 g (¼ cup) double (heavy) cream
1 tablespoon caster (superfine) sugar
small handful of shelled pistachios,
  crushed

Split the vanilla pod open lengthways and scrape out the seeds. Put the seeds, pod and milk into a heavy-based saucepan and bring slowly to the boil, to infuse the vanilla.

Meanwhile, place the egg yolks and sugar in a bowl and mix together for a few seconds, then sift in the flour and mix together. Pour the boiling milk over the yolk mixture, whisking constantly to prevent curdling, then return the mixture to the pan and cook over a medium heat, whisking constantly for about 3 minutes, until nice and thick.

Pass through a fine sieve (strainer), then place a sheet of baking paper or a scattering of caster sugar on the surface of the custard to prevent a skin forming (don't forget to keep your vanilla pod – wash and dry it to use again). Leave the custard to cool, then refrigerate until cold.

Remove the cooled custard from the refrigerator and stir in the roasted pistachio paste until fully combined.

To finish, whip the cream and sugar together until thick, then fold in the chilled custard until well combined. Transfer to a piping bag and you're ready to fill your doughnuts (see page 181)!

When you have piped in the filling, scatter over a few crushed pistachios to decorate.

1 hour 20 minutes
Makes enough to fill
10 doughnuts

Preparation – 15 minutes
Cooling – 1 hour
Finishing – 5 minutes

six

Cakes

Victoria Sponge

A classic Victoria sponge is a true test of a great baker. One of the critical points is to make sure the butter and sugar is really well whipped before adding in the egg. Don't be tempted to open the oven door when baking as this will result in the middle of the cake dropping. It's worth taking the time to butter and flour the cake tin thoroughly, to be sure that the cake pops out cleanly once it has been baked

For the sponge

225 g (8 oz) unsalted butter, softened, plus extra for greasing
225 g (8 oz/1¾ cups) self-raising (self-rising) flour, plus extra for dusting
225 g (8 oz/1 cup) caster (superfine) sugar
4 eggs
1 teaspoon baking powder

For the buttercream

100 g (3½ oz) unsalted butter, softened
150 g (5 oz/1¼ cups) icing (confectioner's) sugar, sifted

To finish

jam of your choice (see page 270 for homemade)
icing (confectioner's) sugar, for dusting

Preheat the oven to 180°C fan (400°F/gas 6). Grease and flour two 20-cm (8-in) round cake tins (pans).

In a large bowl, or in a stand mixer fitted with a paddle attachment, beat the butter and caster sugar until fluffy and very pale in colour. You may need to scrape the sides of the bowl and bring the butter and sugar mixture back to the middle of the bowl before continuing to beat them together. At this point, you can add 2 tablespoons from the total flour amount and mix this into the butter mixture. This helps to stop the mix from splitting when you add the eggs.

Gradually add the eggs, one at a time, beating them into the butter mixture. Make sure each egg is completely incorporated before adding the next.

In a separate mixing bowl, sift together the flour and baking powder. Add to the butter mixture and gently combine, being careful not to overmix at this stage. For a light and fluffy sponge you want to stop mixing as soon as the flour has been evenly incorporated.

Pour the batter into your prepared cake tins and smooth the tops. Bake for 25 minutes, or until a knife inserted into the middle of the sponges comes out clean.

Meanwhile, prepare the buttercream. Combine the softened butter and icing sugar in a mixing bowl (if the icing sugar is quite lumpy you will need to sift it) and beat together until all of the icing sugar has been incorporated and your mix is smooth and thick. You may find it easier to add the icing sugar in two stages.

Remove the baked sponges from the oven and leave to cool on a wire rack. The sponges must cool completely before assembling.

When cool, spread the buttercream over one sponge layer, then spread the jam over the top of the buttercream. Sandwich together with the top layer of sponge. Generously dust the top of your cake with icing sugar, slice and enjoy with a cup of tea.

1½ hours
Serves 6

Preparation – 15 minutes
Baking – 25 minutes
Cooling – 45 minutes
Assembly – 5 minutes

Madeira Cake

In this recipe, we are using a reverse creaming method, which is a way of minimising gluten development in the cake batter. This may feel very back to front, but trust us it works. This is a great base recipe and can be added to and developed with other ingredients, for example desiccated (shredded unsweetened) coconut, pistachio nuts and chocolate chips, etc.

175 g (6 oz) unsalted butter,
   softened, plus extra for greasing
175 g (6 oz/¾ cup) caster (superfine)
   sugar
200 g (7 oz/1½ cups) self-raising
   (self-rising) flour, sifted
50 g (2 oz/½ cup) ground almonds
3 large eggs
1–2 tablespoons full-fat (whole)
   milk (optional)
grated zest of 1 lemon
½ teaspoon almond extract

Optional additions

1–2 tablespoons chopped candied
   peel or glacé cherries
a few prunes, chopped
a few pistachios or hazelnuts,
   chopped

For topping (optional)

flaked (slivered) almonds
Demerara sugar

Preheat the oven to 160°C fan (350°F/gas 4). Grease and line a 900-g (2-lb) loaf tin (pan).

In a large bowl, or in a stand mixer fitted with a paddle attachment, beat the butter and sugar until fluffy and very pale in colour.

In a separate mixing bowl, whisk together the flour and ground almonds until well combined.

Add the dry ingredients to the creamed butter and beat together until all of the dry ingredients have been completely incorporated. You can be fairly vigorous with this if mixing by hand.

Add the eggs to the mixture, one at a time, mixing well between each addition. If you are using a stand mixer, beat the eggs into the mixture on a medium speed. Once you have added all of the eggs, you can increase the speed to high for about 20 seconds until you have a light and creamy batter. If the batter is a little thick, add 1–2 tablespoons of milk until it resembles a very thick pancake batter.

Add the lemon zest, almond extract and any peel, fruits or nuts (if using) and mix to combine.

Pour the cake batter into the prepared tin, and sprinkle with some flaked almonds and Demerara sugar if you like.

Bake for 50–55 minutes, or until the cake is golden and a knife inserted into the middle comes out clean.

Remove from the oven and leave the cake to cool in the tin for 10–15 minutes, then turn it out onto a wire rack, remove the baking paper and leave to cool fully before serving.

1 hour 10 minutes
Serves 6-8

Preparation - 15 minutes
Baking - 50-55 minutes

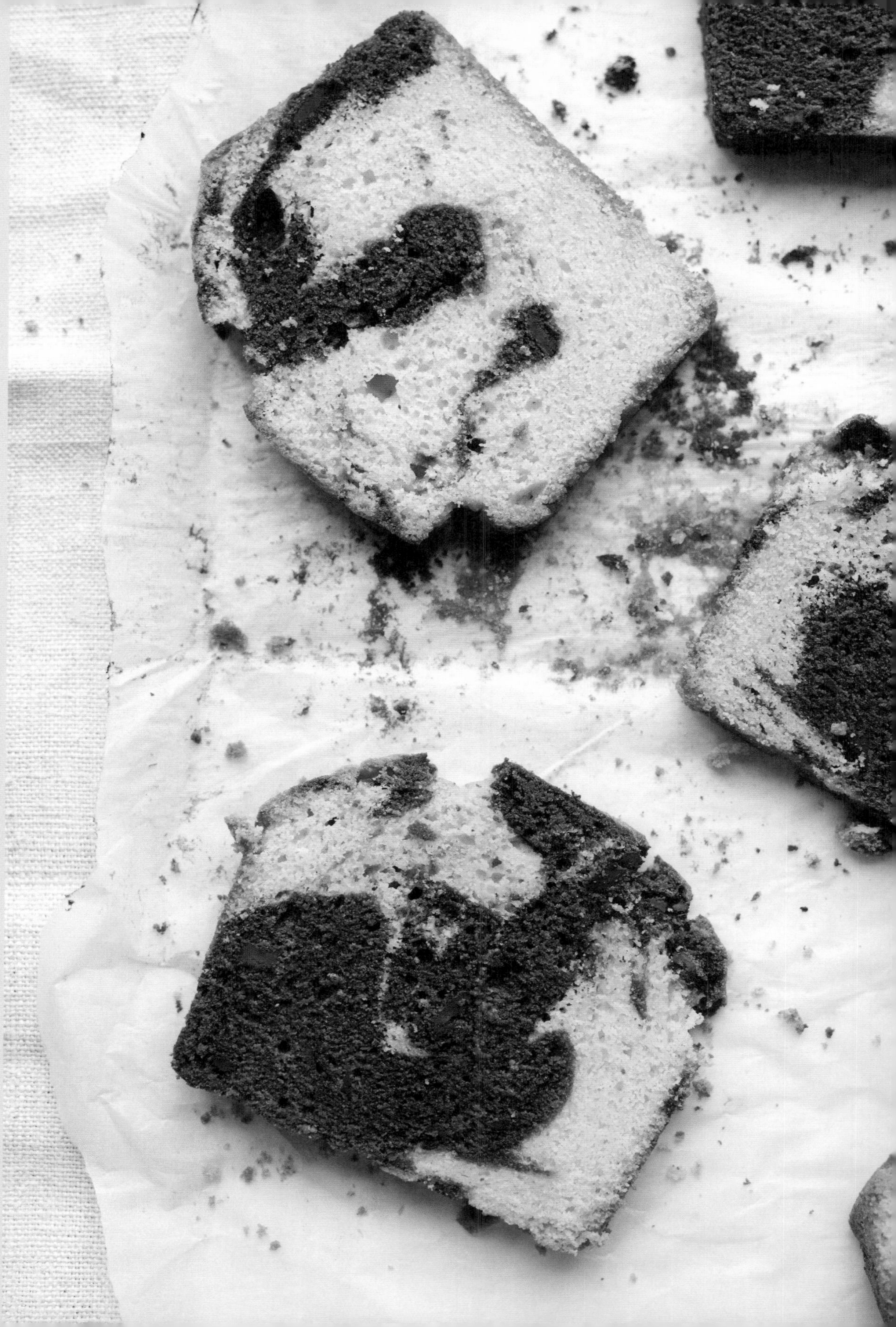

Marble Cake

A very simple, lazy recipe and ideal for family baking – it's a great one to make with children to help them learn the principles of basic cake-baking. By dividing the recipe and adapting part of it, it's amazing how you can achieve two very different flavours from the same batter.

250 g (9 oz) unsalted butter, softened
250 g (9 oz/generous 1 cup) caster (superfine) sugar
4 eggs (225 g/8 oz)
225 g (8 oz/1¾ cups) self-raising (self-rising) flour
4 teaspoons full-fat (whole) milk
pinch of fine sea salt
30 g (1 oz/¼ cup) cocoa powder
handful of chocolate chips (optional)

Preheat the oven to 170°C fan (375°F/gas 5). Grease and line a 900-g (2-lb) loaf tin (pan) with baking paper.

Put all of the ingredients, except the cocoa powder and chocolate chips, into a mixing bowl and beat until everything is completely creamed together and the mixture is smooth. You might find this easier to do in a stand mixer fitted with a paddle attachment.

Divide your batter in half, placing the other half in a separate bowl – it doesn't need to be exact.

Add the cocoa powder and a few chocolate chips to one half of the batter and stir together until well combined.

Add a spoonful of each of the batters to the prepared cake tin, alternating between each batter until you've used them all up and filled the tin. Gently drag a butter knife through the batter in a figure-of-eight shape – this will create the ripple effect in the sponge, but don't overdo it.

Bake for 50 minutes, or until a knife inserted into the middle of the cake comes out clean.

Allow to cool completely before slicing. It's a real delight.

Ginger Cake

We have established a reputation over the years for our classic ginger cake and the recipe has never changed. The important tip is to cook this long and slow, really, the longer the better. This would lend itself to baking in the bottom shelf of an AGA. It is important to activate the bicarbonate of soda (baking soda) with the hot milk when creating the mix. This is critical to the rising process of the bake.

375 g (1½ cups) full-fat (whole) milk
165 g (5½ oz/scant 1 cup) soft dark brown sugar
1 teaspoon bicarbonate of soda (baking soda)
150 g (5 oz) unsalted butter, cubed, plus extra for greasing
85 g (3 oz/3 tablespoons) black treacle (molasses)
165 g (5½ oz/scant ½ cup) golden (light corn) syrup
300 g (10½ oz/generous 2 cups) self-raising (self-rising) flour
2 tablespoons ground ginger
1 teaspoon ground cinnamon
1 teaspoon mixed spice
65 g (2½ oz) stem ginger, chopped
80 g (5 tablespoons) stem ginger syrup from the jar
1 egg, beaten

Pour the milk into a large, heavy-based saucepan, add the sugar and let it dissolve over a medium heat, stirring frequently. Once the sugar has dissolved, increase the heat slightly to bring the milk to scalding point (just below boiling point – when it is ready, small bubbles will appear at the sides and the milk will begin to steam), then remove from the heat and add the bicarbonate of soda – watch out, as it will fizz up a little. Set aside for 10 minutes.

Put the butter, treacle and golden syrup into a medium saucepan set over a medium heat and slowly bring up to a light simmer. All the ingredients should have melted and formed a rich syrup.

Sift the flour and ground spices into a large bowl. Add the syrupy mixture to the flour mixture in 2–3 additions and whisk in. It is quite a dry mixture, so adding the syrup gradually will make it easier to combine. Gradually whisk in the milk mixture until smooth. Finally, add the stem ginger pieces, ginger syrup and egg, and whisk to combine.

Cover the bowl and leave to rest at room temperature for 2 hours. This resting time allows the bicarbonate of soda to activate.

Preheat the oven to 140°C fan (325°F/gas 3). Lightly grease a 26-cm (10-in) springform cake tin (pan) or a 30 x 20-cm (12 x 8-in) traybake tin and line the base and sides with baking paper.

Stir the batter, then pour into the tin.

Bake for about 1 hour, until firm to the touch.

3½ hours
Serves 8-12

Preparation – 30 minutes
Resting – 2 hours
Baking – 1 hour

Carrot Cake

This is the only carrot cake recipe you will ever need. It is super moist and crumbly, and the cream cheese frosting is not too sweet, which creates the perfect balance of flavours. Carrot cake is one of the number-one selling cakes at Bread Ahead, we are always sure to sell out.

200 g (scant 1 cup) sunflower oil, plus extra for greasing
200 g (7 oz/generous 1 cup) soft light brown sugar
3 eggs
200 g (7 oz) carrots, grated
80 g (3 oz/ ⅔ cup) shelled walnuts, chopped
200 g (7 oz/ 1⅔ cups) plain (all-purpose) flour
¾ teaspoon bicarbonate of soda (baking soda)
¾ teaspoon baking powder
¾ teaspoon ground cinnamon
¾ teaspoon ground ginger
¾ teaspoon salt
½ teaspoon vanilla extract

For the frosting

50 g (2 oz) unsalted butter, at room temperature
125 g (4 oz/½ cup) cream cheese, at room temperature
150 g (5 oz/1¼ cups) icing (confectioner's) sugar, sifted
squeeze of lemon juice

To decorate

50 g (2 oz) shelled walnuts, some chopped and some left whole
ground cinnamon

Preheat the oven to 150°C fan (350°F/gas 4). Grease and line a 900-g (2-lb) loaf tin (pan) or a 30 x 20-cm (12 x 8-in) traybake tin.

Put the sugar and eggs into a mixing bowl and whisk vigorously for a few minutes until the mix is well combined, lighter in colour and frothy. Slowly pour in the oil, whisking continuously. Ensure you add the oil very slowly. Whisk for a further 2 minutes until your mixture is creamy and smooth, then add the grated carrots and chopped walnuts and stir to combine.

Sift the flour, bicarbonate of soda, baking powder, cinnamon, ginger and salt into a separate large mixing bowl and whisk to combine.

Add the dry ingredients into the wet mixture along with the vanilla extract, and stir gently to combine.

Pour the mixture into the prepared cake tin and smooth over with a palette knife. Bake for 20–25 minutes, or until golden brown and the sponge bounces back when touched. (If baking in a loaf tin, it may take a little longer – the sponge should be golden, risen and just starting to come away from the sides of the tin.)

Meanwhile, prepare the frosting. In a large bowl, beat the butter until completely smooth, light and fluffy. Next, add in the cream cheese and sifted icing sugar and a little squeeze of lemon juice for flavour. Beat until you have a smooth and creamy frosting. You can chill this in the refrigerator until you're ready to ice your cake.

Leave the cake to cool slightly in the tin before turning out onto a wire rack to cool completely.

When the cake is cold, spread or pipe the cream cheese frosting over the top. Finish with the chopped and whole walnuts and a light sprinkling of ground cinnamon.

Banana Cake

Banana cake is a great way to use up any old speckled or brown bananas. We leave the banana quite chunky, so that you get little bites of it throughout the cake. One of the keys to this recipe's success is to use overripe bananas for a full flavour. Otherwise, this really is a simple one.

210 g (scant 1 cup) vegetable oil, plus extra for greasing
210 g (7 oz/generous 1 cup) soft light brown sugar
2 eggs
1 teaspoon vanilla extract
235 g (8½ oz/1¾ cups) plain (all-purpose) flour
pinch of fine sea salt
1 teaspoon bicarbonate of soda (baking soda)
1 teaspoon baking powder
1 teaspoon ground cinnamon
½ teaspoon ground ginger
2 medium ripe bananas (235 g/8 oz), chopped into 5-mm (¼-in) rounds
Demerara sugar (optional)

Preheat the oven to 170°C fan (375°F/gas 5). Oil and line a 900-g (2-lb) loaf tin (pan) with baking paper. This sponge has a habit of sticking, even to silicone paper. I recommend lightly brushing the baking paper with oil, too, to make it super-non-stick.

Put the sugar, eggs and vanilla into a mixing bowl and whisk vigorously for a few minutes until well combined, lighter in colour and frothy. Slowly pour in the oil, whisking continuously. Ensure you add the oil very slowly. Whisk for a further 2 minutes until your mixture is creamy and smooth.

In a separate bowl, sift together the dry ingredients, then add to the wet mixture along with the chopped bananas. Mix until just combined – you don't want to see any streaks of flour.

Pour the batter into the prepared loaf tin. Before baking, you can add a sprinkle of Demerara sugar over the top for extra crunch, if you like.

Bake for about 1 hour 10 minutes until golden brown.

Let cool, then slice and enjoy!

Swiss Roll

Swiss roll is a bit of a tricky one. It's important to whisk the eggs very stiff before folding in the flour. It's also important not to overbake the sponge, so that it stays nice and moist and will be easy to roll. As with all cakes and pastries, using homemade jam will always give the most delightful results.

vegetable or sunflower oil, for greasing
4 eggs
120 g (4 oz/generous ½ cup) caster (superfine) sugar, plus extra for dusting
1 teaspoon vanilla extract
80 g (3 oz/⅔ cup) self-raising (self-rising) flour

For the filling

200 g (1 cup) double (heavy) cream
1 teaspoon vanilla extract
jam of choice (see page 270 for homemade)
200 g (7 oz) raspberries (optional)

Preheat the oven to 170°C fan (375°F/gas 5). Line a 23 x 33-cm (9 x 13-in) Swiss roll tin (pan) with baking paper and lightly brush with oil.

In a large mixing bowl, or in a stand mixer fitted with a whisk attachment, whisk the eggs, sugar and vanilla extract until very pale, fluffy and thickened. Sift in the flour, then carefully fold it in, ensuring that you don't knock out the air you've worked so hard to incorporate.

Pour the batter into the prepared tin and smooth with a spatula until evenly spread.

Bake for 10–12 minutes, or until just firm to the touch.

Place a sheet of baking paper, or a clean dish towel, slightly bigger than the tray, over the work surface and dust with caster sugar. Turn the sponge out onto the paper or towel, then peel off the baking paper on the bottom of the sponge. While the sponge is still warm, start rolling it up from a short end, keeping the paper/towel inside the roll. Keep rolling until the whole sponge is fully rolled up. Set aside and allow to cool completely.

Meanwhile, prepare the filling. In a large mixing bowl, whip the cream and vanilla extract until they form soft peaks.

Once the sponge has cooled, gently un-roll it. Spread the whipped cream over the sponge, then pipe or spoon the jam across the cream in rows. Sprinkle over the raspberries, if using.

Take the longest edge of the sponge and, using the baking paper/towel to help you, roll up the sponge quite tightly, making sure the filling stays inside. Dust the Swiss roll with extra caster sugar and cut into slices to serve.

1 hour
Serves 6-8

Preparation - 10 minutes
Baking - 10-12 minutes
Cooling - 30 minutes
Assembly - 5 minutes

Black Forest Gateau

This is a bit cheesy and very kitsch – but, my goodness, it is disgracefully delicious. A retro classic that deserves a place in the hall of fame, it's quite hard to find a version of this dessert made really well, but it is actually extremely simple. It's advisable to make the cherry compote the day before. We've put the kirsch as an optional ingredient but classically you would always use it. Visually, it's a showstopper.

vegetable or sunflower oil,
    for greasing
6 eggs
175 g (6 oz/¾ cup) caster (superfine)
    sugar
120 g (4 oz/1 cup) self-raising
    (self-rising) flour
60 g (2 oz/½ cup) cocoa powder

To decorate

1 x recipe quantity Cherry Compote
    (see page 274), adding 50 ml
    (3 tablespoons) kirsch, to taste

For the whipped cream

250 g (1¼ cups) double
    (heavy) cream
60 g (2 oz/¼ cup) caster
    (superfine) sugar

Tip

It is important to bake the sponge batter immediately after mixing, as it will start to lose volume.

Preheat the oven to 180°C fan (400°F/gas 6). Grease and line two 23 x 33-cm (9 x 13-in) Swiss roll tins (pans).

In a large mixing bowl (or in a stand mixer fitted with the whisk attachment), use an electric whisk to whisk the eggs and sugar together until light, frothy and thickened (about 12 minutes on high speed). The mixture should have increased in volume by about four times.

Sift together the flour and cocoa powder and gently fold into the egg mixture, being careful not to knock out the air.

Pour the batter into your prepared tins and spread it gently into the corners.

Bake for 15 minutes until springy to the touch.

Remove from the oven and allow to cool completely.

If you haven't made it already, prepare the cherry compote according to the method on page 274, adding a little kirsch to taste.

Whip the cream and caster sugar together until thickened. Transfer to a piping bag and refrigerate until needed.

Cut the cooled sponges in half down the middle, so you have four equal-sized rectangles.

Spread 2 tablespoons of the compote over the first layer of sponge (we find it best to do this when the compote is still a little runny), then spread a quarter of the whipped cream over the top. Repeat with the next two sponge layers, placing the final layer of sponge on top. For the top layer, pipe rosettes of whipped cream around the edge and fill the middle with the remaining cherry compote.

1 hour 10 minutes   Preparation – 15 minutes   Cooling – 30 minutes
Serves 8   Baking – 15 minutes   Assembly – 10 minutes

Cassata Siciliana

This is an unusual, but deeply satisfying, dessert. The sponge is super light and airy, the ricotta is rich and creamy and the citrus fruit and chocolate flavours pop on the palate delightfully. I also like this dessert because it's not overwhelmingly sweet but hits all the right notes. The cake is much easier to work with if you bake the sponge the day before you intend to assemble it.

For the sponge

vegetable oil, for greasing
6 eggs
180 g (6 oz/generous ¾ cup) caster (superfine) sugar
1½ teaspoons vanilla extract
120 g (4 oz/generous ¾ cup) self-raising (self-rising) flour

For the filling

500 g (1 lb 2 oz/2¼ cups) ricotta
150 g (5 oz/⅔ cup) caster (superfine) sugar
150 g (5 oz/scant 1 cup) dark chocolate chips
150 g (5 oz/scant 1 cup) finely chopped Candied Fruits (see page 273)

To finish

icing (confectioner's) sugar, for dusting
175 g (6 oz) marzipan (you can colour it with a few drops of green food colouring if you like)
Candied Fruits (see page 273), for decorating

Stage 1

Start with the sponge. Preheat the oven to 180°C fan (400°F/gas 6). Lightly oil and line two 22-cm (9-in) round springform cake tins (pans) with baking paper.

In a large mixing bowl, or in a stand mixer fitted with a whisk attachment, whisk the eggs, sugar and vanilla extract until very pale, fluffy and thickened. Sift the flour into the egg mixture and carefully fold in, ensuring that you don't knock out the air you've worked so hard to incorporate.

Pour the batter into the prepared tins and smooth with a spatula until evenly spread. Bake for 12–16 minutes, or until just firm to the touch.

Remove the baked sponges from the oven and allow them to cool before removing them from their tins.

To prepare the filling, place the ricotta in a fine-mesh sieve (strainer) and leave to drain for 10 minutes.

Transfer the drained ricotta to a bowl, add the sugar and beat until smooth. Add the chocolate chips and chopped candied fruits and mix until well combined. If you are assembling the cake the following day, store the filling in the refrigerator. It will be easier to assemble the cake if all the components are completely chilled.

Stage 2

Line the inside of one the empty springform tins with clingfilm (plastic wrap) or a generous dusting of icing sugar to prevent the marzipan from sticking.

Roll out the marzipan to about 4-mm (¼-in) thick and slice it into a long strip, wide enough to completely line the inside edge of the tin and allowing for a little excess to stand higher than the rim. Carefully line the tin with it.

---

3 hours (or 2 days)
Serves 10

Stage 1
Preparation - 25 minutes
Baking - 10-12 minutes
Chilling - 1 hour or overnight (optional)

Stage 2
Assembly - 15 minutes
Chilling - 1 hour

Place one of the sponge layers into the marzipan-lined tin (you may need to gently trim the edges to help it fit). Spread the ricotta filling over the sponge and top with the second sponge layer. Carefully trim any excess marzipan so that it is level with the top of the sponge, or gently tuck it over the top edge of the sponge. Cover and place in the refrigerator to set for at least 1 hour.

When ready to serve, remove the cake from the refrigerator, gently remove it from the tin, dust liberally with icing sugar and decorate the top with some more candied fruit.

Simnel Cake

A simnel cake is quite a niche product, nonetheless we feel it important to honour these baking traditions at Bread Ahead. As we are situated just 30 yards from Southwark Cathedral, we try to embrace as many baking traditions stemming from religious holidays as possible. It's also really nice to take the opportunity to explore the heritage in these bakes.

1 x Fruit Cake (see Christmas Fruit
   Cake on page 256)
250 g (9 oz) marzipan (see page 254
   or use store-bought)
icing (confectioner's) sugar,
   for dusting
jam (see page 270 for homemade),
   for brushing

Make the cake according to the instructions on pages 256–257.

When ready to decorate, divide the marzipan into two even blocks.

Lightly dust the work surface with icing sugar and roll one half of the marzipan into a circle slightly larger than your cake. Using the cake tin (pan) as a guide, place it on top of the marzipan and use a sharp knife to cut around the edge of the tin. This will give it a nice sharp edge.

Lightly brush the top of your cake with a little jam (this will help the marzipan stick) and carefully place the marzipan circle onto the cake.

Divide the remaining block of marzipan into 11 even amounts. Roll each piece between your palms to form 11 smooth balls. Evenly place the marzipan balls around the edge of the cake (you can brush a little jam under each ball to help them stick).

For a really traditional finish, take a blowtorch and lightly brûlée the top of the marzipan, or place it under a hot grill (broiler) for a few minutes, but keep an eye on it!

2 days
Serves 12

Day 1

Preparation - 5 minutes
Soaking - overnight

Day 2

Preparation - 20 minutes
Baking - 1 hour 30-40 minutes
Cooling - 2 hours
Decorating - 10 minutes

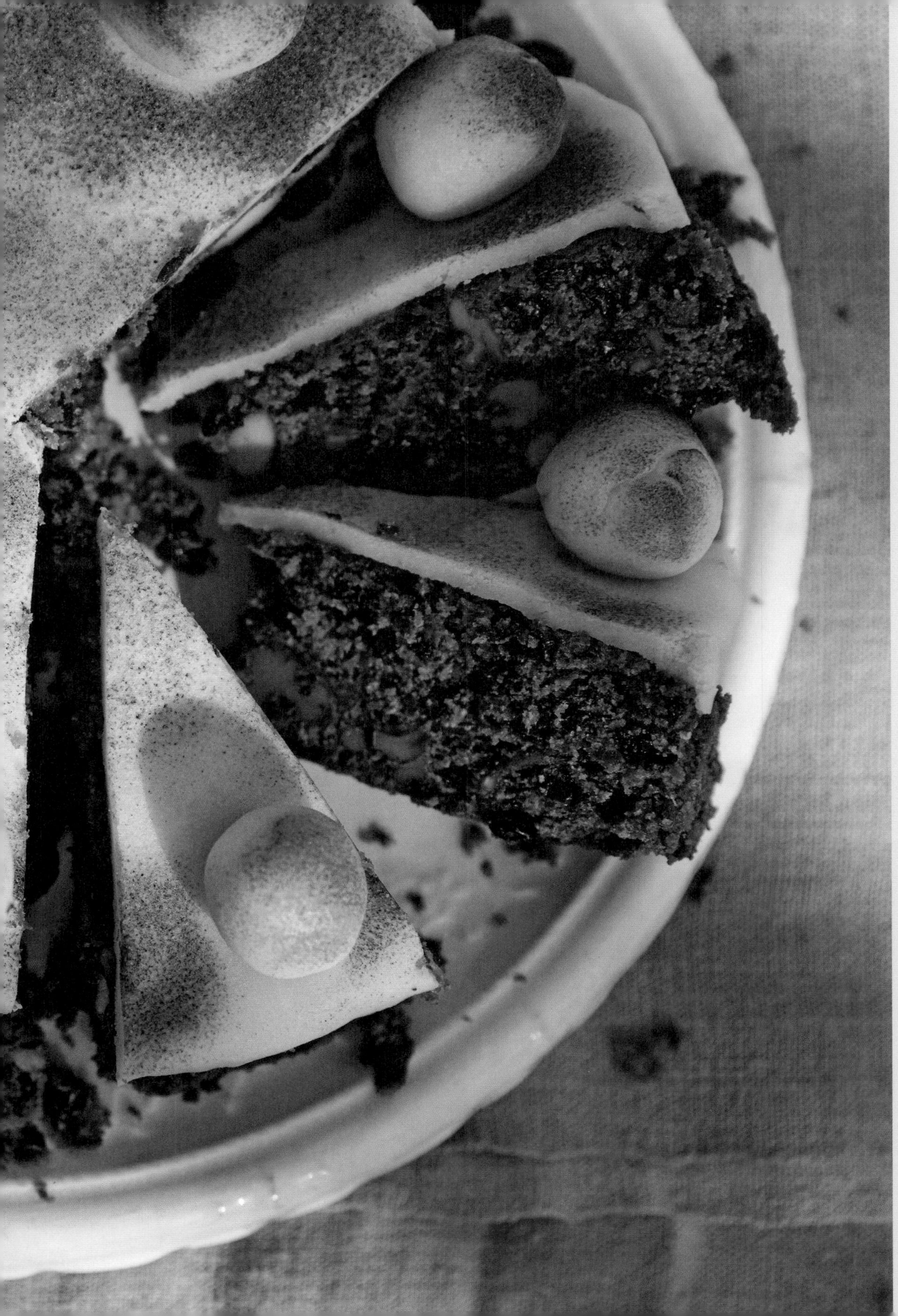

seven

Cookies

Chocolate Chip Cookies

Another great family bake, one of the beauties of choc chip cookies is that they have a very quick turnaround time. You can make these from start to finish in just 30 minutes. Cookies are best eaten when they're still warm, so keep the cookie dough stored in the refrigerator or freezer and bake them as you need them. Always bake them so they are still a little gooey in the middle.

75 g (2½ oz) unsalted butter, softened
45 g (1¾ oz/scant ¼ cup) caster (superfine) sugar
90 g (3¼ oz/scant ½ cup) soft light brown sugar
1 egg, beaten
175 g (6 oz/scant 1½ cups) plain (all-purpose) flour
3 g (1 teaspoon) baking powder
3 g (1 teaspoon) bicarbonate of soda (baking soda)
1 g (⅛ teaspoon) fine sea salt
150 g (5 oz/scant 1 cup) chocolate chips
flaky sea salt, for sprinkling (optional)

Preheat the oven to 180°C fan (400°F/gas 6) and line a baking sheet with baking paper.

In a large mixing bowl, cream the butter and sugars together until light and fluffy and almost white in colour. This stage is key as it adds a wonderfully soft texture to the finished cookie.

Add the egg slowly and continue to beat until completely incorporated.

In a separate bowl, sift together the flour, baking powder, bicarbonate of soda and salt.

Add the dry ingredients to the creamed butter along with the chocolate chips and gently bring together until just combined. Overmixing at this stage is not only unecessary, but more importantly it can toughen the dough.

Divide the dough into six pieces, about 100 g (3½ oz) each, and shape into balls. Place the dough balls on the baking sheet, leaving space in between each one as the cookies will spread as they bake. Press down on the top of each ball to flatten it slightly. Dip your fingers in some water and gently dimple the top of the cookie dough. You can also add a sprinkling of flaky sea salt, if you wish.

Bake for 12 minutes for a soft middle.

Tip

You can keep your raw cookie dough in a sealed container in the refrigerator for up to a week and bake as needed. Nothing beats a freshly baked cookie still warm from the oven.

Banana and Chocolate Chip Cookies

It took around 20 attempts to get this recipe just right. The key thing is to really whip up the butter and sugar at the start. These are showstoppers. The milk chocolate is sweet but it works really well with the creaminess of the banana.

75 g (2½ oz) unsalted butter, softened
125 g (4 oz/generous ½ cup) caster (superfine) sugar
1 egg, beaten
225 g (8 oz/1¾ cups) plain (all-purpose) flour
3 g (1 teaspoon) baking powder
3 g (1 teaspoon) bicarbonate of soda (baking soda)
2 g (¼ teaspoon) fine sea salt
175 g (6 oz/1 cup) milk chocolate chips
1 banana, chopped

Preheat the oven to 180°C fan (400°F/gas 6) and line a baking sheet with baking paper.

In a large mixing bowl, cream the butter and sugar together until light and fluffy and almost white in colour. This stage is key as it adds a wonderful soft texture to the finished cookie.

Add the egg slowly and continue to beat until completely incorporated.

In a separate bowl, sift together the flour, baking powder, bicarbonate of soda and salt. Add the dry ingredients and chocolate chips to the creamed butter and gently bring together until just combined.

Finally, fold in the chopped banana. Be careful not to overmix, just bring the dough together.

Divide the dough into six pieces, about 100 g (3½ oz) each, and shape into balls.

Place the dough balls on the baking sheet, leaving a little space in between each one as the cookies will spread as they bake. Press down on the top of each dough ball to flatten it slightly.

Bake for 12 minutes for wonderfully soft cookies.

Choc Hazelnut/ White Choc and Cranberry Cookies

This is such a versatile cookie recipe, you can add all sorts of additions to make it your own. Here are two of our favourites. Chocolate and hazelnut is a classic combination, but feel free to swap out the hazelnuts for walnuts, pecans or macadamias. Alternatively, tart cranberry and sweet creamy white chocolate make a perfect pair.

75 g (2½ oz) unsalted butter, softened
135 g (4½ oz/scant ⅔ cup) caster (superfine) sugar
1 egg, beaten
225 g (8 oz/1¾ cups) plain (all-purpose) flour
3 g (1 teaspoon) baking powder
3 g (1 teaspoon) bicarbonate of soda (baking soda)
1 g (⅛ teaspoon) fine sea salt

For Choc Hazelnut Cookies

175 g (6 oz/1 cup) milk chocolate chunks
75 g (2½ oz/scant ⅔ cup) hazelnuts, chopped

For White Choc and Cranberry Cookies

175 g (6 oz/1 cup) white chocolate chips
75 g (2½ oz/scant ⅔ cup) dried cranberries, chopped

Preheat the oven to 180°C fan (400°F/gas 6) and line a baking sheet with baking paper.

In a large mixing bowl, cream the butter and sugar together until light and fluffy and almost white in colour. This stage is key as it adds a wonderful soft texture to the finished cookie.

Add the egg slowly and continue to beat until completely incorporated.

In a separate bowl, sift together the flour, baking powder, bicarbonate of soda and salt. Add the dry ingredients to the creamed butter and gently bring together until just combined. The mixture will look fairly dry to begin with, but continue to chop through the mixture with your spoon and it will come together as a smooth mixture after a couple of minutes.

Finally, fold in your chosen additions. Be careful not to overmix, just bring the dough together. You may find it easier to get your hands in at this stage to bring the dough together.

Divide the dough into six pieces, about 120 g (4 oz) each, and shape into balls.

Place the dough balls on the baking sheet, leaving a little space in between each one as the cookies will spread as they bake. Press down on the top of each dough ball to flatten it slightly.

Bake for 12 minutes for a soft middle.

Palets Bretons (French Salted Butter Biscuits)

These are a bit special. It's worth using a really good-quality butter if you can, you will notice the difference. Much like a cookie dough you can store this dough in the refrigerator or freezer and bake as needed. These are great served with a strong coffee or espresso.

2 egg yolks
90 g (3¼ oz/generous ⅓ cup) caster (superfine) sugar
140 g (4½ oz) unsalted butter, softened
155 g (5 oz/1¼ cups) plain (all-purpose) flour
5 g (scant 1 teaspoon) fine sea salt
5 g (1½ teaspoons) baking powder

In a large mixing bowl, whisk together the egg yolks and sugar until the sugar is dissolved. Add the softened butter and beat in with a wooden spoon until the mixture is light and fluffy and slightly paler in colour.

In a separate mixing bowl, sift together the flour, salt and baking powder.

Add the dry ingredients to the creamed butter and mix for about 2 minutes until you have a smooth, well-combined dough. There should be no traces of flour left in the dough.

Remove the dough from the mixing bowl and bring it together into a sausage shape. Wrap in baking paper and chill in the refrigerator for 1 hour.

Preheat the oven to 170°C fan (375°F/gas 5).

Remove the chilled dough from the refrigerator and slice into nine 'pucks', each about 50 g (2 oz). Place each puck of dough into the individual holes of a silicone or metal muffin pan. Baking in a mould gives these biscuits that lovely, authentic, crisp edge.

Bake for 20 minutes until golden and crisp.

Cool on a wire rack.

eight

Desserts

Apple Crumble

The trick to a really good apple crumble is a really chunky, shortbread-style topping. We've used a mixture of apples, which helps to achieve acidity and a chunky texture in the apple base. When in season, a few blackberries or gooseberries are delicious to add a little more tartness. I like to bake an apple crumble quite well, so there's almost a little caramelisation around the edges of the pan.

2 eating apples (Granny Smith are ideal)
2 Bramley apples
100 g (3½ oz/scant ½ cup) Demerara sugar, or to taste
1–2 cloves
1 teaspoon ground cinnamon

For the crumble topping

150 g (5 oz/1¼ cups) plain (all-purpose) flour
80 g (3 oz/⅓ cup) caster (superfine) sugar
150 g (5 oz) unsalted butter, softened
100 g (3½ oz/1 cup) ground almonds

Preheat the oven to 160°C fan (350°F/gas 4).

Peel the apples, remove the cores and cut into 1-cm (½-in) chunks. Place in an ovenproof baking dish and toss with the Demerara sugar and spices.

Add all of the crumble topping ingredients to a mixing bowl. Using your fingertips, rub the butter into the dry ingredients to form a rough crumb. There's no need to make a perfectly fine crumb – some big chunks of crumble will be lovely.

Sprinkle the crumble topping over the apples.

Bake for 30–35 minutes until your crumble is beautifully golden and bubbling.

Allow the crumble to cool for a few minutes before serving, ideally with homemade custard.

Spotted Dick

My mum always made spotted dick and as children we found it rather comical. Nonetheless, there is something extremely satisfying about this humble British classic. As with the jam roly poly, I like a sprinkle of caster sugar and either custard or a little pouring cream.

240 g (8½ oz/scant 2 cups) self-raising (self-rising) flour
pinch of salt
120 g (4 oz/1 cup) shredded suet (or grated frozen vegetable shortening)
70 g (2½ oz/scant ⅓ cup) caster (superfine) sugar, plus extra to serve
150 g (5 oz/1¼ cups) currants or raisins
a little grated nutmeg, plus extra to serve
pinch of finely grated lemon zest
pinch of finely grated orange zest
175 g (¾ cup) full-fat (whole) milk
unsalted butter, for greasing

Add the flour, salt, suet, sugar, currants or raisins, nutmeg, lemon and orange zests to a large mixing bowl and stir to combine. Make a well in the middle of the dry ingredients and pour in the milk, then bring the mixture together to form a rough, sticky dough.

To cook in a pudding bowl, grease a 450-g (1-lb) pudding bowl with plenty of butter and pour your batter into the bowl, pressing it down gently with the back of a spoon. Cover the bowl with a small square of baking paper and then a large square of kitchen foil over the top, pressing the foil around the edges of the bowl to seal it.

Take a large saucepan with a lid and place the pudding inside. Fill the pan with water until it reaches three-quarters of the way up the sides of the bowl. Steam over a medium heat for 1½ hours. You may need to top up the water occasionally.

Alternatively, if your oven has a steam function, preheat it to 160°C (325°F) and steam bake for 1 hour and 20 minutes.

Carefully remove the pudding from the pan, leave it to cool for a few minutes before carefully peeling back the foil and baking paper. Your pudding should have a lovely golden crust and a knife inserted into the middle should come out clean.

Slice the pudding and serve with a generous dusting of sugar, some freshly grated nutmeg and a very generous helping of fresh custard.

45 minutes
Serves 4-6 (depending on how greedy you are)

Preparation - 10 minutes
Baking - 1 hour 20-30 minutes

Tips

- Feel free to use your favourite spices – allspice and mace also work very well in place of the ginger.

- You can also purée the dried fruits if you want a smoother consistency to your pudding.

- If the water is still very hot when adding the bicarbonate of soda, it can react quickly and spill over – keep another saucepan to hand, or you can use a larger saucepan in the first instance to boil the water.

Sticky Toffee Pudding

The sticky toffee pudding originated in the Sharrow Bay hotel in Cumbria. I am fortunate enough to have been there and eaten it many years ago. This is our version as theirs is a closely guarded secret. I like to leave the dates and apricots a little bit chunky. Walnuts can also be added, which really brings something extra to it. I like a spoonful of extra-thick Jersey cream alongside.

100 g (3½ oz) unsalted butter, at room temperature, plus extra for greasing
100 g (3½ oz) dates
100 g (3½ oz) dried apricots
150 g (5 oz/generous ¾ cup) soft dark brown sugar
2 eggs
175 g (¾ cup) water
1 teaspoon bicarbonate of soda (baking soda)
100 g (scant ½ cup) full-fat (whole) milk
200 g (7 oz/1½ cups) self-raising (self-rising) flour
1–2 teaspoons ground ginger (to taste)

For the sticky toffee sauce

200 g (7 oz/generous 1 cup) soft dark brown sugar
100 g (3½ oz) unsalted butter
100 g (scant ½ cup) double (heavy) cream
50 g (2 oz/2 tablespoons) black treacle (molasses)

Preheat the oven to 160°C fan (350°F/gas 4). Grease 12 individual pudding moulds or a 900-g (2-lb) loaf tin (pan).

Soak the fruits in a little water so they soften slightly, then roughly chop. If your fruits are quite dry, we recommend simmering them in a pan of water until they absorb some of the water and begin to soften. Remove from the heat and allow to cool, then roughly chop.

In a mixing bowl, cream together the butter and dark brown sugar. You're looking for a creamy consistency and for the mixture to become much paler, along the lines of a light caramel. Add the creamed butter and sugar to the purée and stir to combine. Add the eggs and stir to combine.

Add the measured water to a small saucepan and bring to the boil, then remove from the heat and leave to rest for 20 seconds. Add the bicarbonate of soda to the pan and gently stir until it has dissolved entirely, then add to the butter mixture. This process activates the bicarbonate of soda and allows the pudding to rise. Stir the water and butter together until combined, then add the chopped fruit and milk. Stir together.

In a separate bowl, sift together the flour and ground ginger, then fold through the wet mixture. Be careful not to overmix – you just want to bring the dry and wet ingredients together.

Pour the batter into the prepared moulds or tin. If using individual moulds, place them on a baking sheet. Bake for 20–25 minutes (this will depend on the size of the mould you are using).

Meanwhile, prepare the sticky toffee sauce. Add all the sauce ingredients to a saucepan and stir gently over a medium heat until melted, then bring to the boil and continue cooking over a high heat for about 3 minutes. Continue to stir the sauce as it cooks so that it doesn't stick to the bottom of the pan. The sauce will bubble like a caramel when it's ready.

Serve the puddings with the sauce immediately – simply perfect.

Jam Roly Poly

Back to school with this one. Everybody has a place in their heart for a jam roly poly. It works exceptionally well with raspberry jam, but damson, blackberry or gooseberry are also particularly delicious. I like to sprinkle a little caster sugar on top and serve with a little pouring cream or custard.

220 g (8 oz/1⅔ cups) self-raising (self-rising) flour, plus extra for dusting
110 g (3¾ oz/scant 1 cup) shredded suet (or grated frozen vegetable shortening)
1 tablespoon caster (superfine) sugar, plus extra for dusting
good pinch of salt
150 g (scant ⅔ cup) full-fat (whole) milk or water, at room temperature
150 g (½ cup) jam of choice (we like raspberry – see page 270 for homemade)

Preheat the oven to 180°C fan (400°F/gas 6).

Put the flour and shredded suet into a large mixing bowl and use your hands or a dough scraper to crumble the suet through the flour until it is broken down and well mixed into the flour. Add the sugar and salt and stir to combine. Make a well in the middle of the mixture and pour in the milk or water, then bring all of the ingredients together into a rough dough.

Tip the dough onto a very lightly floured work surface and gently knead, just enough to bring the dough together. With a rolling pin, roll out the dough into a 30-cm (12-in) square, about 5-mm (¼-in) thick, dusting with flour so the dough doesn't stick to the work surface.

Spread the jam over the surface of the dough, leaving a clear border of 1–2 cm (½–¾ in) around the edges. Now, roll the dough up as you would a Swiss roll.

Cut a sheet of baking paper and one of kitchen foil, each about 30 x 40 cm (12 x 16 in), and lay the sheet of baking paper on top of the sheet of foil.

Place the roll of dough, seam-side down, in the middle of the baking paper. Carefully but firmly, roll the paper around the dough, encasing it like a Christmas cracker. Repeat with the foil, encasing the baking paper and dough. Firmly twist the foil at either end to seal.

Place a baking tray on the bottom of the oven and carefully fill halfway with boiling water. Place the parcel onto a baking sheet and place on the middle shelf of the oven. Bake for 35–40 minutes.

Carefully remove from the oven and peel away the foil and baking paper. Your roly poly should be lovely and springy and cooked all the way through. Generously dust the top with caster sugar, slice and serve with fresh custard.

Queen of Puddings

This is an opportunity to excel in piping and presentation. I like to whip the meringue to very stiff peaks so that the topping of the pudding can be very spiky like the points of a crown. It is opulent and decadent as a dessert, yet made with very humble ingredients.

For the custard

unsalted butter, softened,
 for greasing
550 g (2¼ cups) full-fat (whole) milk
grated zest of 1 lemon
70 g (2½ oz/scant 1 cup) fresh
 breadcrumbs
3 egg yolks
45 g (1¾ oz/scant ¼ cup) caster
 (superfine) sugar

For the cheat's filling

150 g (5 oz/scant ½ cup) raspberry
 jam (see page 270 for homemade)
60 g (2 oz) fresh or frozen
 raspberries

For the meringue

3 egg whites
160 g (5½ oz/scant ¾ cup) caster
 (superfine) sugar

Preheat the oven to 150°C fan (350°F/gas 4). Grease an ovenproof dish or a deep 25-cm (10-in) cake tin (pan) with butter.

For the custard, add the milk and lemon zest to a saucepan set over a medium heat and warm to scalding point (just below boiling). Add the breadcrumbs, stir to combine, then remove from the heat.

In a large mixing bowl, whisk together the egg yolks and sugar. Pour over the hot milk and whisk to combine.

Pour the custard into the prepared tin and bake for 30 minutes or until just set. It can have a slight wobble in the middle. Leave to cool.

Meanwhile, make the cheat's filling. Add the jam and raspberries to a saucepan set over a medium-high heat and bring to the boil, then reduce the heat to a simmer. Stirring occasionally, leave the filling mixture to thicken, then remove from the heat and leave to cool.

Meanwhile, make the meringue. Place a clean heatproof bowl over a saucepan of simmering water (do not let the base of the bowl touch the water). Add the egg whites and half of the sugar to the bowl and whisk vigorously to stiff peaks. Remove from the heat, add the remaining sugar and continue to whisk for several minutes until the meringue becomes very glossy and thick. Transfer to a piping bag, if wished.

Preheat the grill (broiler) to its highest setting.

Pour the cooled raspberry filling over the cooked custard base, then pipe or spoon the meringue over the raspberry layer. It's important that the custard and jam layers are fairly cool, as you don't want to melt the uncooked meringue.

Place the meringue-topped pudding under the hot grill and cook for about 5–8 minutes until the meringue is crisp and browned all over. Keep a close eye on it.

Allow to cool slightly before serving.

1½ hours
Serves 8

Preparation – 10 minutes
Baking – 30 minutes
Cooling – 30 minutes
Finishing – 20 minutes

ANATOMY OF QUEEN
OF PUDDINGS

peaked 'crown'
of marshmallowy
meringue

deep, rich filling
with plenty of
home-made jam

moist, creamy
custard

Eve's Pudding

A lovely autumnal classic that's great for a beginner, this dish can be created in just over an hour. It's the perfect finish to a Sunday lunch, served with lashings of custard.

100 g (3½ oz) unsalted butter, softened, plus extra for greasing
4–6 large Bramley apples (about 1 kg/2 lb 4 oz)
4 tablespoons Demerara sugar, or to taste
½ teaspoon ground cloves (or your favourite spice)
100 g (3½ oz/scant ½ cup) caster (superfine) sugar
3 eggs
150 g (5 oz/1¼ cups) self-raising (self-rising) flour
pinch of salt
1–2 tablespoons full-fat (whole) milk (optional)

To finish

Demerara sugar (optional)
flaked (slivered) almonds (optional)

Preheat the oven to 180°C fan (400°F/gas 6). Liberally grease a large ovenproof dish (about 2–3-litre/8–12-cup capacity) with butter.

Peel and chop the apples into 1-cm (½-in) cubes. Add to the prepared dish along with the Demerara sugar and spice and toss to coat the apple pieces. Bake for 10 minutes until softened slightly.

Meanwhile, in a large mixing bowl, or in the bowl of a stand mixer fitted with a paddle attachment, cream the butter and caster sugar together until light and fluffy and much paler in colour. Add 1 egg and mix until fully incorporated, then add about a third of the flour and the salt and continue mixing. Continue alternating between eggs and flour until they are all incorporated and the batter is smooth and fairly thick. If it is too thick, add a little milk until it reaches a nice dropping consistency.

Spread the batter over the now softened apple, spreading it to all corners of the baking dish and ensuring all of the apples are covered. Sprinkle with a generous helping of Demerara sugar or flaked almonds over the top, if you like.

Bake for a further 30–40 minutes, or until golden brown.

Remove from the oven and cool slightly before serving with custard.

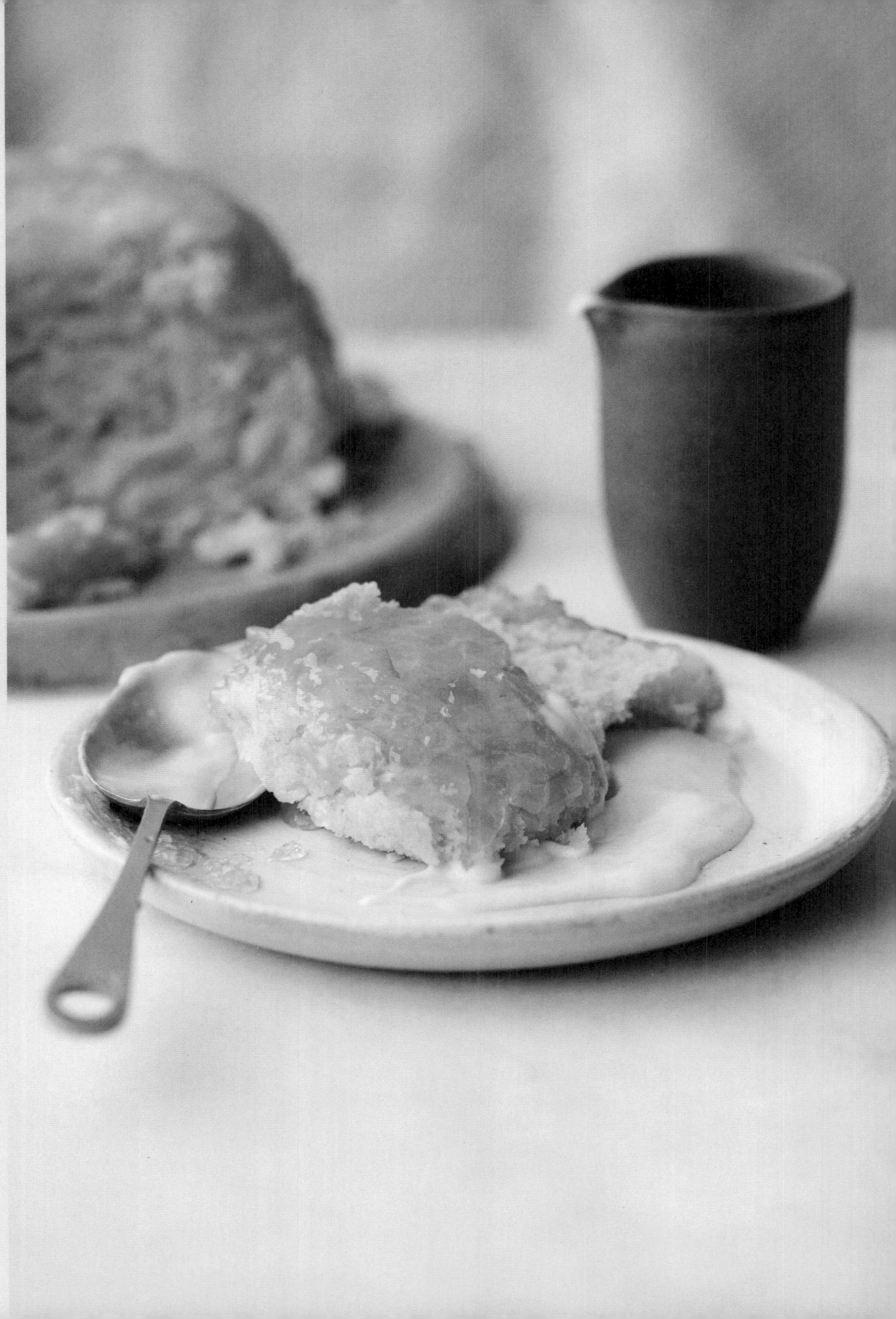

Steamed Marmalade Pudding

I can't make this pudding without thinking of Paddington Bear. That said, the marmalade does bring a lovely bitterness, which makes it an unusual dessert in that it's not overly sweet. I would say this is quite a grown-up, proper pudding.

butter, for greasing
240 g (8½ oz/scant 2 cups) self-raising (self-rising) flour
pinch of salt
120 g (4 oz/1 cup) shredded suet (or grated frozen vegetable shortening)
70 g (2½ oz/scant ⅓ cup) caster (superfine) sugar
a little grated nutmeg, plus extra to serve
finely grated zest of ½ lemon
finely grated zest of ½ small orange
150 g (scant ⅔ cup) full-fat (whole) milk
2 heaped tablespoons marmalade (or jam/compote of choice) (see Chapter 10 for homemade versions)

Lightly grease a 900-g (1-lb) pudding bowl.

Combine the flour, salt, suet, sugar, nutmeg, lemon and orange zest in a large mixing bowl, stirring to combine. Make a well in the middle and pour in the milk, then bring the mixture together to form a rough dough.

Spoon the marmalade into the base of the bowl and pour the pudding mixture in on top. Smooth the surface of the pudding and cover with a circle of baking paper. Cover the top of the bowl with a layer of kitchen foil, tucking it around the edges to seal in the steam as it bakes.

Place the bowl inside a large saucepan with a lid. Fill the pan with water until it reaches three-quarters of the way up the sides of the bowl. Steam the pudding over a medium heat for 1 hour 20 minutes. You may need to top up the water occasionally.

Carefully remove the pudding from the pan and leave it to cool for a few minutes before carefully peeling back the foil and baking paper. Place a plate over the bowl and carefully turn the plate and bowl upside down. The pudding should release – if it doesn't, run a sharp knife around the edges of the bowl.

Slice the pudding and serve with some freshly grated nutmeg and a very generous helping of fresh custard.

Cherry Clafoutis

Clafoutis Limousin comes from the Auvergne region of France, which is known for its exceptional cherries. For best results, use really plump, juicy cherries when they're in season, but frozen cherries or fresh blueberries and apricots work really well, too. Ideally, serve this straight from the oven, when it is still souffléd up around the edges.

butter, for greasing
3 eggs
100 g (3½ oz/scant ½ cup) caster (superfine) sugar, or to taste, plus extra to sprinkle
60 g (2 oz/½ cup) plain (all-purpose) flour
pinch of salt
120 g (½ cup) full-fat (whole) milk
120 g (½ cup) double (heavy) cream
1 teaspoon almond extract
zest of ½ orange
280 g (10 oz/1½ cups) fresh (or frozen) cherries, pitted
15 g (3 tablespoons) flaked (slivered) almonds
icing (confectioner's) sugar, to decorate
extra-thick cream, to serve

Preheat the oven to 180°C fan (400°F/gas 6). Grease a 1-litre (4-cup) baking dish with butter.

Put the eggs and sugar into a mixing bowl and whisk together until well combined. Add the flour and salt and whisk until smooth. Finally, add the milk, cream, almond extract and orange zest and mix until you have smooth, lump-free batter. Now, give the batter a really good whisk.

Pour the batter into the prepared baking dish, scatter over the cherries and flaked almonds and scatter a generous sprinkling of caster sugar over the top.

Bake for 24 minutes until the top is golden. The clafoutis should have risen and have lovely crisp edges. If the top is browning too quickly, remove from the oven and place a sheet of kitchen foil over the baking dish and return the clafoutis to the oven until cooked.

Remove from the oven and serve immediately, dusted with icing sugar, with some extra-thick cream.

35 minutes
Serves 4–6

Preparation – 10 minutes
Baking – 24 minutes

Crème Caramel

Each of these recipes takes me to a moment in my career. I first made crème caramel when I was working as a pastry chef at Bibendum with Simon Hopkinson. The key to making a really good one is the caramel – it needs to be really dark, which gives a lovely bittersweet flavour. Another addition to this recipe, which works exceptionally well, is a little orange zest boiled in the milk. When cooking these, a low oven is essential.

For the custard

1 vanilla pod
800 g (3¼ cups) full-fat (whole) milk
200 g (scant 1 cup) double (heavy) cream
3 eggs, plus 3 egg yolks
150 g (5 oz/⅔ cup) caster (superfine) sugar

For the caramel

200 g (7 oz/scant 1 cup) granulated or caster (superfine) sugar
100 g (scant ½ cup) water, plus 3 tablespoons

Preheat the oven to 120°C fan (275°F/gas 1).

To make the custard, spilt the vanilla pod lengthways and use the back of a knife to gently scrape out the seeds. Add the seeds and pod along with the milk and cream to a heavy-based saucepan set over a medium heat and bring to a simmer. Remove from the heat.

In a large mixing bowl, whisk together the eggs, egg yolks and sugar until frothy and pale.

Place a fine mesh sieve (strainer) over the mixing bowl and pour the warm milk mixture through the sieve to catch the vanilla pod. Ensure the milk mixture is not too hot, as this will scramble the eggs. Gently whisk together until you have a smooth custard.

To make the caramel, add the sugar and 100 g (scant ½ cup) of water to a large, heavy-based saucepan. Bring to the boil and allow the mixture to take on a dark caramel colour. There should be no need to stir it.

Remove from the heat and add a further 3 tablespoons of water to the saucepan. Do so very carefully as the caramel will likely bubble and boil up.

Return the saucepan to the heat and bring back to the boil, then remove it from the heat. This will form a thick caramel that will set beautifully.

Place six small ramekins or one large ovenproof dish (glass or metal dishes work just as well as ceramic) into a large roasting tin (pan). Pour the caramel into the ramekins/dish, then slowly and carefully pour the custard mixture over the top of the caramel. Place the roasting tin into the preheated oven, then carefully fill the tin with a 2-cm (¾-in) depth of water.

Bake for 1 hour–1 hour 20 minutes (depending on the size of your dishes). When ready, the custard should still have a slight wobble in the middle.

Remove from the oven and allow to cool in the refrigerator for 4 hours.

Turn out and devour, perhaps with a little pouring cream.

Tip

Remember to save vanilla pods and add them to a jar of sugar to really enhance the flavour of your bakes.

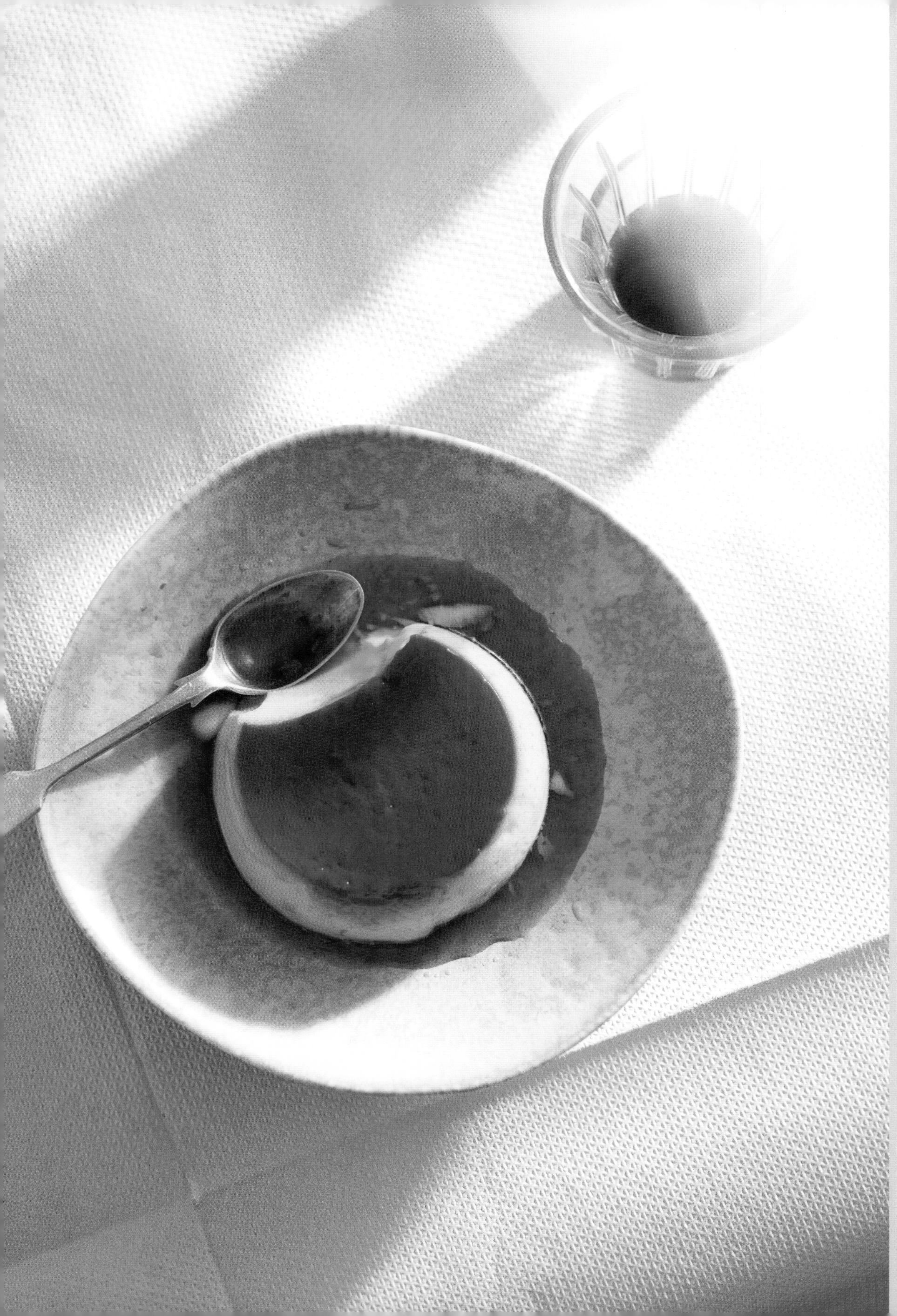

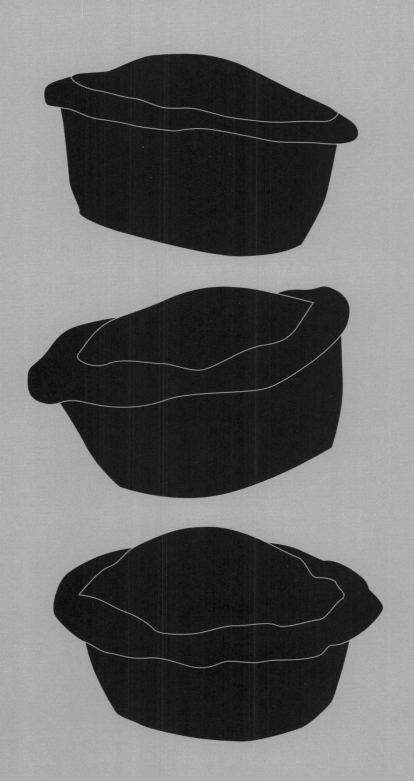

nine

Christmas

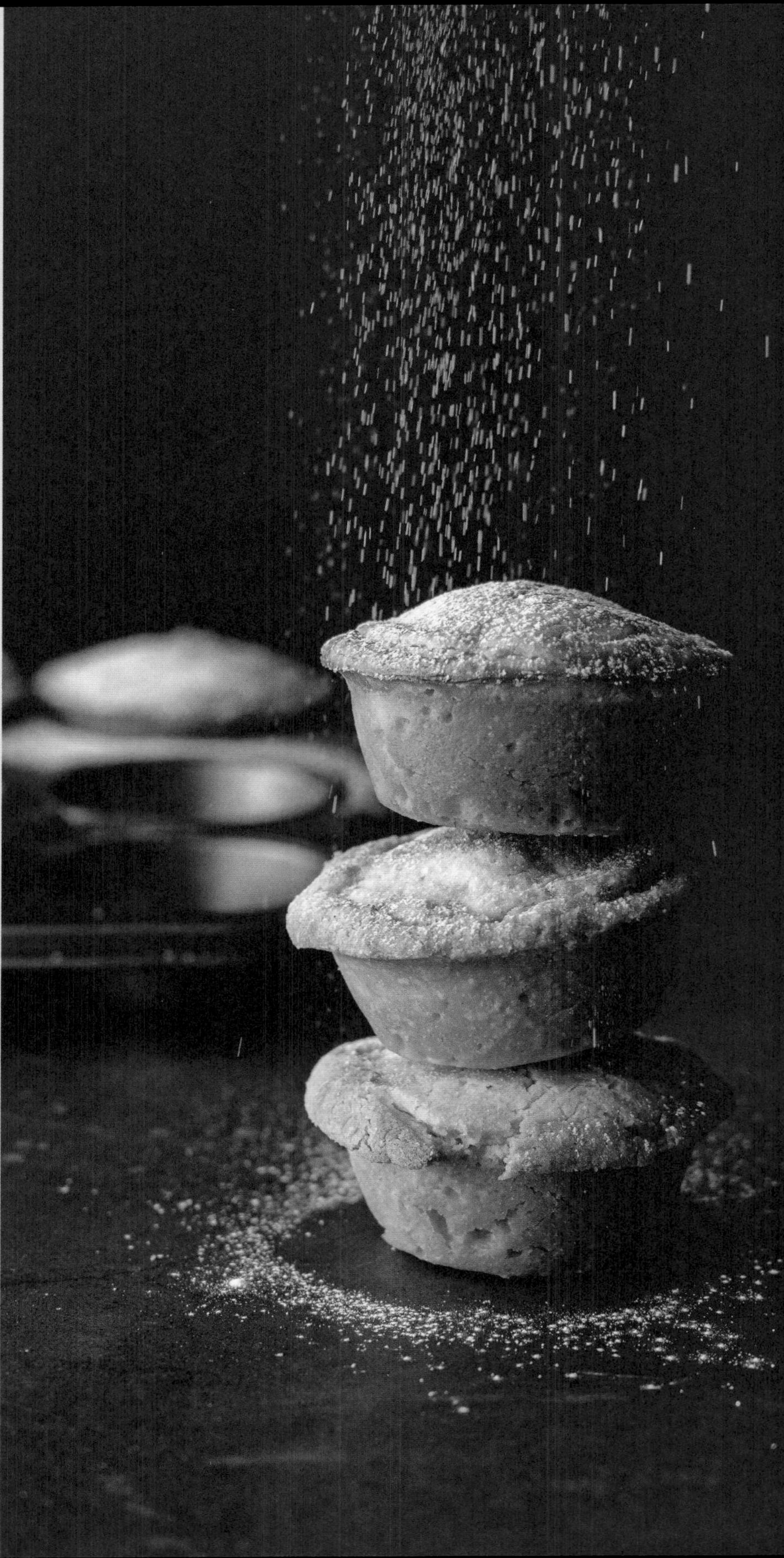

Mince Pies

If you've never enjoyed a freshly baked homemade mince pie piping hot from the oven, you haven't truly experienced the joy of Christmas. I only make these at Christmastime, as they're such a treat, served just warm, with cold extra-thick cream.

375 g (13 oz/2⅔ cups) strong white (bread) or plain (all-purpose) flour, plus extra for dusting
150 g (5 oz/⅔ cups) caster (superfine) sugar
pinch of fine sea salt
225 g (8 oz) cold unsalted butter, cubed, plus extra for greasing
1 egg plus 1 egg yolk
1 x recipe quantity Bread Ahead Mincemeat, to fill (see page 281)
1 egg, beaten, to glaze
2 tablespoons Demerara sugar

Place the flour, caster sugar and salt into a mixing bowl and whisk to combine. Add the butter and rub it in with your fingertips. It's important to use very cold butter to prevent it melting into the flour. Shake the bowl from time to time to bring the remaining lumps of butter to the surface and continue rubbing in. Once you have achieved breadcrumb consistency, add the egg and yolk and bring the pastry together to a rough dough.

Turn the dough out onto the work surface and gently bring it together, giving it a few gentle folds to ensure all of the ingredients have been incorporated. Roll the dough into a ball and flatten a little into a disc. Wrap in baking paper and chill in the refrigerator for 30 minutes.

Preheat the oven to 160°C fan (350°F/gas 4), and butter and flour a 12-hole muffin tray (pan). Remove the pastry from the refrigerator and let it soften a little.

Roll out the pastry on a lightly floured work surface to 4–5-mm (¼-in) thick. Remember to give the pastry quarter turns as you roll it, dusting your work surface with extra flour to ensure the pastry doesn't stick.

Cut out 12 circles for the base of the pies with a 10-cm (4-in) round pastry cutter and 12 circles for the tops with a 7-cm (3-in) cutter, re-rolling the pastry when necessary.

Line the holes in the muffin tray with the larger circles of pastry, letting them overhang. Spoon about 3 heaped tablespoons of mincemeat into each one and cover with the smaller circles. Brush the tops of the pies with the beaten egg, then bring up the overhanging pastry around the sides to create a seal around the top of each pie. Sprinkle with Demerara sugar and cut a small slit in the top of each pie to let the steam escape.

Bake for about 40 minutes until golden brown.

Leave the pies in the tray for 5 minutes, then remove carefully, releasing them all the way around first with a small knife. Place on a wire rack to cool, although they are best served warm or immediately.

Tip

You can leave the dough in the refrigerator for up to 5 days. However, you will need to take it out 1 hour before you intend to roll it, to allow it to come up to room temperature. You can also store it in the freezer for up to 3 months.

1 hour 40 minutes
Makes 12

Preparation - 10 minutes
Chilling - 30 minutes
Assembly - 15-20 minutes
Baking - 40 minutes

Stollen

The stollen shape represents the swaddled baby Jesus. As a lover of marzipan, I am rather partial to a slice of stollen. This recipe is quite classical in its approach, but at the same time simple enough for the average home baker to get a really pleasing result. This will keep well in a tin for 2–3 weeks.

100 g (scant ½ cup) milk, warmed to room temperature
15 g (3 teaspoons) fresh yeast or 8 g (2½ teaspoons) dried yeast
35 g (1¼ oz) egg (about ⅔ egg)
zest of 1 lemon
250 g (9 oz/scant 2 cups) strong white (bread) flour
30 g (1 oz/2 tablespoons) caster (superfine) sugar
3 g (½ teaspoon) fine sea salt
50 g (2 oz) unsalted butter, softened and cubed
40 g (1½ oz/¼ cup) whole blanched almonds
90 g (3¼ oz/ ¾ cup) raisins or currants
45 g (1¾ oz/¼ cup) mixed peel
2 g (¾ teaspoon) ground cardamom
2 g (¾ teaspoon) grated nutmeg
icing (confectioner's) sugar, for dusting

For the marzipan

200 g (7 oz) store-bought marzipan or to make your own:
100 g (3½ oz/1 cup) ground almonds
100 g (3½ oz/scant 1 cup) icing (confectioner's) sugar
zest of ½ small orange
1 egg white
½ teaspoon rose water

For the syrup glaze

100 g (3½ oz/scant ½ cup) caster (superfine) sugar
80 g (5 tablespoons) water
1 tablespoon rum (optional)

In a small bowl, combine the warm milk and the yeast, stirring with your hand to dissolve. Add the egg and lemon zest and whisk in.

In a large bowl, combine the flour, sugar and salt. Add the butter and rub in with your fingers to breadcrumbs. Make a well in the middle, add the yeast mixture and bring together, with a dough scraper if possible, into a rough dough.

Empty the dough onto the work surface. Make sure you are left with a clean bowl. Knead for 4 minutes until the dough becomes slightly less sticky, smooth and more elastic. Push the dough out into a rough square, spread the almonds, raisins, peel and spices over the surface and gently fold the dough over to enclose them. Continue to gently knead the dough, working the fruits and nuts into it. When they are evenly distributed and the dough is no longer sticky, return the dough to the bowl. Cover with a plate, shower cap or damp dish towel and leave to prove at room temperature for 1–2 hours, or until risen and springy.

Meanwhile, prepare your marzipan if making your own, so that it has time to chill. Combine the ground almonds, icing sugar and orange zest in a large bowl. Add the egg white and rose water, and mix to a stiff dough. Wrap in baking paper and chill for at least 1 hour.

Preheat the oven to 150°C fan (350°F/gas 4). Line a baking sheet with baking paper.

Press the dough out into a rectangle, about 20 x 24 cm (8 x 9½ in). Roll the marzipan into a rope, 24-cm (9½-in) long. Place it in the middle of the of the dough and fold over the dough to encase it, leaving a large lip on one side – this is the classic stollen shape. Press down the edges to completely enclose the marzipan.

Place the stollen on the lined baking sheet and bake for 40 minutes.

Meanwhile, prepare the syrup glaze. Put the sugar, water and rum, if using, into a small saucepan and bring to the boil. Simmer for 2 minutes, then remove from the heat.

Remove the stollen from the oven and brush it generously with the syrup. Let the stollen sit in the syrup and absorb it as it cools. Leave to cool completely, then dust with icing sugar to serve.

3-4 hours
Serves 12

Preparation – 25 minutes
Proving/Chilling – 1-2 hours

Baking – 40 minutes
Cooling – 1 hour

Christmas Fruit Cake

I do believe that we have now created the perfect Christmas cake. This took years and years of practice. The base is a great classic fruit cake that we also use for our Simnel Cake (page 216) and make two months in advance for all of the flavours to mature and develop. It's important to soak the dried fruits in the fruit juice for at least 24 hours beforehand, to get them plump and juicy. It has a long, slow cooking time, which will help you to achieve a really moist, dense cake.

We decorate our Christmas cakes generously with just about every fruit and nut we can get our hands on. They are designed to be the jewel in the crown of the Christmas table.

For the fruit cake

200 g (7 oz/generous 1½ cups) raisins
200 g (7 oz/generous 1½ cups) sultanas (golden raisins)
200 g (7 oz/1⅓ cups) currants
200 g (7 oz/generous ¾ cup) prunes, roughly chopped
100 g (3½ oz/½ cup) dried cherries
50 g (2 oz/¼ cup) mixed peel
400 g (generous 1½ cups) orange juice
125 g (½ cup) vegetable oil, plus extra for greasing
115 g (4 oz) unsalted butter, softened
150 g (5 oz/generous ¾ cup) soft dark brown sugar
200 g (7 oz/generous 1 cup) soft light brown sugar
30 g (1 oz/1½ tablespoons) black treacle (molasses)
3 large eggs (180 g/6½ oz)
250 g (9 oz/scant 2 cups) plain (all-purpose) flour
6 g (2 teaspoons) baking powder
5 g (scant 1 teaspoon) salt
5 g (scant 1 tablespoon) allspice
5 g (scant 1 tablespoon) ground cinnamon
5 g (scant 1 tablespoon) ground nutmeg
10 g (1½ tablespoons) mixed spice
300 g (10½ oz/3 cups) walnuts

Day 1

Combine the dried fruits with the orange juice in a large mixing bowl, stirring well. Cover and leave to soak overnight at room temperature.

Day 2

Preheat the oven to 140°C fan (325°F/gas 3). Lightly oil and line a 23–24-cm (9–9½-in) cake tin (pan) with a double layer of baking paper.

Add the butter and sugars to a large mixing bowl or the bowl of a stand mixer fitted with the beater attachment and cream together until fluffy and a light caramel colour. Slowly add the vegetable oil, beating constantly, until you have a smooth homogenous mixture, then beat in the treacle. Add the eggs, one at time, beating until each is incorporated before adding the next. Add the soaked fruits and stir well until all of the fruits are evenly distributed.

Sift the dry ingredients into a separate bowl, then add to the wet ingredients along with the walnuts. Stir until everything is combined – you don't need to mix too thoroughly, but make sure there are no streaks of flour and that the fruit is evenly distributed.

Pour the batter into the tin and smooth the top with the back of a spoon. Cover the tin with a layer of kitchen foil and bake for 1 hour, then remove the foil, return the cake to the oven and bake for a further 30–40 minutes.

Leave to cool in the tin. When the cake is completely cool, remove the baking paper and re-wrap in clean baking paper or clingfilm (plastic wrap). It will keep in an airtight container (a metal biscuit tin is ideal as plastic can sweat) for up to 3 months.

---

2 days
Serves 12

Day 1
Preparation – 5 minutes
Soaking – overnight

Day 2
Preparation – 20 minutes
Baking – 1 hour 30–40 minutes
Cooling – 2 hours
Decorating – 10 minutes

To decorate

icing (confectioner's) sugar,
   for dusting
125 g (4 oz) marzipan (see page 254
   or use store-bought)
jam (see page 270) or candied fruit
   syrup (see page 273), for brushing
Candied Fruits (see page 273)
nuts of choice

To decorate, lightly dust the work surface with icing sugar and roll the marzipan into a circle or square slightly larger than your cake. Using the cake tin as a guide, place it on top of the marzipan and use a sharp knife to cut around the tin. This will give it a nice sharp edge.

Lightly brush the top of your cake with a little jam or some candied fruit syrup and carefully place the marzipan onto the cake.

Layer over the candied fruits and nuts. You can either do this in rows, alternating between rows of fruit and nuts, or arrange a single layer of candied fruits and stud the nuts in between.

Finish with a generous glaze of candied fruit syrup or some jam diluted with a little water.

Yule Log

This is one of the favourite workshops at the Bread Ahead Bakery School. There are a few critical points to pay attention to, as with all baking, but the results are generally excellent. This is a perfect solution for gluten-free Christmas baking. We recommend using a stand mixer to whisk up the eggs, this is a key step and will give a lovely light and airy finish to the sponge.

For the sponge

unsalted butter, for greasing
6 eggs, separated
150 g (5 oz/⅔ cup) caster (superfine) sugar
50 g (2 oz/scant ½ cup) cocoa powder, plus extra for dusting
1 teaspoon vanilla extract (optional)

For the buttercream

175 g (6 oz) dark chocolate, chopped
225 g (8 oz) unsalted butter, softened
250 g (9 oz/2 cups) icing (confectioner's) sugar
1 teaspoon vanilla extract

To finish

2 tablespoons icing (confectioner's) sugar or cocoa powder

Preheat the oven to 160°C fan (350°F/gas 4). Line a 23 x 33-cm (9 x 13-in) Swiss roll tin with baking paper and grease with butter.

In a large mixing bowl, or the bowl of a stand mixer fitted with a whisk attachment, whisk the egg whites until stiff. Ensure your bowl is clean and dry, as any moisture or grease will affect the whipping of your egg whites. Add 50 g (2 oz/¼ cup) of the caster sugar and continue whisking until the peaks hold their shape.

In a separate bowl, whisk the egg yolks with the remaining sugar until the mixture is glossy and holding its shape (ribbon stage). If using a stand mixer, empty the whipped egg whites into a separate bowl, then add the egg yolks and remaining caster sugar to the now empty bowl of your mixer and whisk as described.

Add the cocoa powder and vanilla, if using, to the yolk mixture, using a metal spoon to fold it in. Ensure you do this slowly to avoid knocking out the air. Then, carefully fold half of the egg whites into the chocolate mixture, again slowly folding the mixture to maintain the air. Once you've incorporated the first half, fold in the remaining egg whites.

Slowly pour the batter into the prepared tin, carefully spreading the mixture into the corners.

Bake for 20 minutes.

Remove the sponge from the oven and allow to sit for a few minutes before turning it out. Lay a sheet of baking paper or a clean dish towel on the work surface and dust with caster sugar. Turn the sponge out onto the baking paper or towel, then peel off the baking paper on the bottom of the sponge. While it is still warm, roll the sponge up along the shortest side towards you, using the paper or towel to ease the rolling. Set aside to cool completely.

Meanwhile, make the buttercream. Melt the chocolate in a bowl set over a pan of simmering water, ensuring the bottom of the bowl is not touching the water. Once melted, remove the bowl from the heat and allow to cool.

1 hour 20 minutes
Serves 8

Preparation – 15 minutes
Baking – 20 minutes
Cooling – 30 minutes
Assembly – 15 minutes

In a separate bowl, cream together the butter and icing sugar until pale and fluffy, then add the melted chocolate and vanilla and mix until well combined, light and glossy.

Unroll your cooled sponge and spread a thin layer of the buttercream on the inside, then roll the sponge back up as tightly as you can (if it cracks that's fine, as you are going to cover it with buttercream).

Place the sponge roll on a cake board and use a palette knife or butter knife to spread the remaining buttercream over the whole cake. For a traditional yule log design, take a fork and drag the teeth along the buttercream to create bark-like lines. Sift icing sugar or cocoa powder over the yule log to finish.

Christmas Pudding

This recipe actually came to me from my mum. Mum's recipes are always best. This Christmas pudding is really moist and crumbly. One of the important details is using fresh breadcrumbs as they help to create a lovely texture. It's good to make the pudding around 2–3 months in advance to allow the fruit to mature. Don't forget to make a wish when you're stirring the mix – a year is a long time to wait for the next one.

50 g (2 oz) blanched almonds
1 large Bramley apple
300 g (10½ oz) prunes
100 g (3½ oz) candied peel
400 g (14 oz/3¼ cups) raisins
400 g (14 oz/3¼ cups) currants
140 g (4½ oz/generous 1 cup) plain (all-purpose) flour
100 g (3½ oz/1¼ cups) fresh breadcrumbs
100 g (3½ oz/½ cup) soft dark brown sugar
½ nutmeg, grated
1 tablespoon mixed spice
3 large eggs
2 tablespoons brandy or Cognac, plus extra for flaming
250 g (9 oz/2 cups) shredded suet (or grated frozen vegetable shortening)
unsalted butter, softened, for greasing

Start by preparing the fruits and nuts for the pudding: Roughly chop the whole almonds into coarse nibs. Peel and chop the apple into 5-mm (¼-in) cubes (they don't need to be perfect, but we like the fruits to be roughly the same size). Roughly chop the prunes to the same size. If your mixed peel is in strips, finely chop it – there's no need to chop if it is already finely diced.

Put all the ingredients except the suet into a large mixing bowl. Stir once or twice to roughly combine. Add the suet to the bowl in thirds, stirring well between each addition. Stir for a few minutes until you can see the suet is evenly distributed throughout the mixture.

Grease two 1.2-litre (4¾-cup) pudding moulds with softened butter and line the bottom of each with a circle of baking paper.

Fill the moulds generously with the pudding mixture, packing it in tightly.

Cover the tops of each mould with another circle of baking paper slightly larger than the mould – you need enough excess paper to fold around the top of each mould and secure with string. You can cover the tops of each pudding with another large circle of kitchen foil and secure with string or create a foil 'parcel' around the entire mould.

Place your puddings inside a large saucepan with a lid. Fill the pan with enough water to reach three-quarters of the way up the sides of the moulds. Steam your puddings on a medium-low heat for 8 hours. You may need to top up the water occasionally.

Remove the pan from the heat, carefully remove the puddings and leave them to cool overnight.

When the puddings are cold, remove the foil and paper layers. Wrap the puddings in a new layer of baking paper and kitchen foil and secure with string. Store in a cool, dry place until you are ready to serve.

To serve, boil or steam each pudding for 1 hour and turn out onto a plate. You can, if you like, flame the pudding with a tablespoon of rum or brandy.

8½ hours, plus overnight resting, plus 1 hour finishing
Makes 2 puddings

Preparation – 30 minutes
Cooking – 8 hours
Cooling – overnight
Finishing – 1 hour

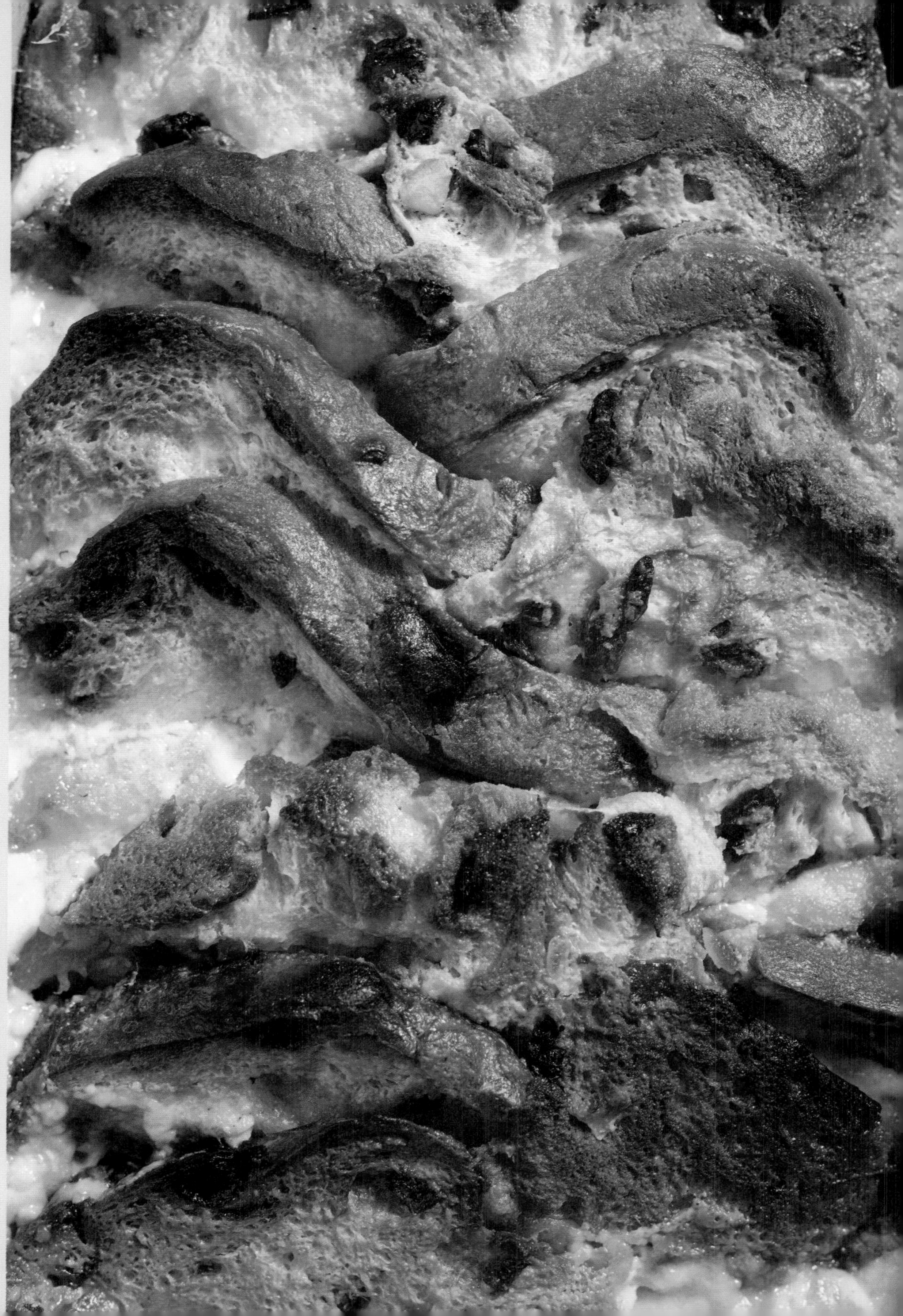

Panettone Pudding

I can't think of another bread that represents Christmas more than a panettone. This pudding is a great way to use up any leftover slices. Although we're not making panettone in this book, there are some great artisan panettone readily available at Christmastime that will work perfectly.

60 g (2 oz) unsalted butter, cubed
1 store-bought loaf of panettone
    (about 500 g/1 lb 2 oz)
250 g (1 cup) double (heavy) cream
250 g (1 cup) full-fat (whole) milk
4 egg yolks
100 g (3½ oz/scant ½ cup) caster
    (superfine) sugar
zest of ½ orange
zest of ½ lemon
good pinch of ground nutmeg

Grease a large casserole dish with half of the butter.

To prepare the panettone, slice the loaf into pieces about 1-cm (½-in) thick. Either slice the pieces in half or into quarters, depending on the size of your loaf. Layer the bread in the casserole dish.

In a mixing bowl, whisk together the cream, milk, egg yolks, sugar, zests and nutmeg until well combined.

Pour the custard mixture over the bread, ensuring every piece is well coated. Leave the pudding to soak for about 30 minutes.

Meanwhile, preheat the oven to 160°C fan (350°F/gas 4).

Dot the top of the pudding with the remaining butter and bake for 35 minutes until golden and the edges of the bread have gently caramelised.

Leave the pudding to cool for about 30 minutes.

Serve with custard or (dare we say it) a dash of fresh cream, if you can handle a little more.

1 hour 45 minutes   Preparation – 10 minutes   Baking – 35 minutes
Serves 6   Resting – 30 minutes   Cooling – 30 minutes

Galette des Rois

Classically eaten on Epiphany in France, we make these in the bakery exclusively for this celebration. We even include the figurine and crown for a fully authentic experience. The most common decoration is a classic geometric spiral, although there are some very elaborate creations out there. This is essentially a very simple bake, but makes for a central element on the table of Epiphany.

600 g (1 lb 5 oz) Puff Pastry
   (see pages 134–137)
plain (all-purpose) flour, for dusting
1 egg, beaten
400 g (14 oz) Frangipane
   (see page 111)

Roll out the pastry on a lightly floured work surface into a large circle, 4-mm (¼-in) thick. Remember to turn the pastry and dust with flour as you roll it to ensure it doesn't stick.

If making individual galettes, cut out four discs using a 10-cm (4-in) round pastry cutter, then cut out a further four discs with a 12-cm (5-in) round cutter.

If making one large galette, cut out two discs, using 26-cm (10-in) and 30-cm (12-in) cake tins (pans) as guides to cut around.

Spread the frangipane into the middle of the smaller disc/s and gently flatten it out very slightly. Place the larger disc/s over the top and carefully tuck the top layer around the base, creating a clean seal all the way around.

Place onto a lined baking sheet, then cover and chill in the refrigerator for 2–3 hours.

Preheat the oven to 180°C fan (400°F/gas 6).

Generously glaze the pastry/pastries with beaten egg. You need to glaze the pastry before scoring so that you can create a precise pattern. Using a sharp knife, score a pattern of your choice on top.

Bake for 25–28 minutes for the small, or 30–32 minutes for the large, until the pastry is golden and the middle is cooked right through.

Serve with extra-thick Jersey cream – this is a very decadent dessert!

ten

Jams & Preserves

Seville Orange Marmalade

We are very fortunate to be based in Borough market, which is overflowing with seasonal produce. Every year, I make one large batch of marmalade as soon as the first delivery of Seville oranges arrives at the market, usually in late January. You can use any variety of oranges, but there's nothing quite like a Seville orange, so do take the time to visit the market, if you can.

750 g (1 lb 10 oz) Seville oranges (if you can find them)
1 lemon
1.5 kg (3 lb 5 oz/7½ cups) sugar (caster/superfine, granulated or preserving sugar)
1 litre (4 cups) water

Stage 1

Place the whole oranges and lemon in a large saucepan and cover with enough water so that they are completely submerged. Set the saucepan over a high heat and bring to the boil, then reduce the heat to medium, cover the pan with a lid and simmer for 2 hours.

Remove the saucepan from the heat and allow the oranges and lemon to cool completely in the water.

Stage 2

Once the oranges and lemon are completely cold, remove them from the water and drain in a colander. They should be quite soft at this point. Slice them in half and scoop out the cooked flesh, including the pips, and place in a large saucepan. Reserve the peels for later.

Add the sugar and measured water (or enough water to cover the sugar) to the saucepan with the orange and lemon pulp. Stir, then set the saucepan over a high heat and bring to a rolling boil. Cook the pulp mixture for about 40 minutes until it reaches 105°C (221°F) on a sugar thermometer.

Meanwhile, use a sharp knife to finely shred the orange and lemon peels into thin strips.

When the pulp mixture has reached temperature, remove it from the heat and very carefully pass it through a sieve (strainer) set over a large mixing bowl. Using the back of a ladle, push the pulp through the sieve.

Return the sieved mixture to the saucepan along with all of the shredded peel. Set over a medium-high heat and bring to the boil, then gently bring the mixture up to 105°C (221°F) on the thermometer, stirring frequently to ensure it doesn't burn or stick.

When your marmalade is ready, pour it into sterilised jars (see page 13) and seal securely with lids. You can do this with a ladle or use a jug to pour the marmalade into the jars. Store in the refrigerator for up to 3 months.

4½ hours
Makes 3 x 330-g (11-oz) jars

Stage 1
Preparation - 2 minutes
Cooking - 2 hours
Cooling - 1 hour

Stage 2
Preparation - 30 minutes
Cooking - 1 hour

Classic Jams

Jam is best made with freshly picked seasonal fruit. This is not always possible, so fresh berries will be absolutely fine and frozen do actually make a fair replacement. We find the best berries are raspberry, blackberry and blueberry as these all have quite a lot of natural acidity. As this jam has no preservatives, it's best kept in the refrigerator.

500 g (1 lb 2 oz/4 cups) raspberries (or berries of choice)
450 g (1 lb/2 cups) caster (superfine) sugar
juice of 1 lemon
5 g (1 teaspoon) pectin powder (or ½ apple, see tip, below)

Place a plate in the refrigerator or freezer to get cold.

Put all of the jam ingredients into a heavy-based saucepan set over a medium heat and stir together. Once the sugar has dissolved, bring to the boil, then reduce the heat and simmer for 5 minutes until thickened.

To test whether your jam has reached setting point, take 1 teaspoon of the jam and place it on the cold plate. Allow to cool, then run your finger through it. If this leaves a clear run and the jam doesn't run back in on itself, the setting point has been reached.

Alternatively, once the jam is boiling, you can use a digital thermometer to measure the temperature. It will be ready when it reaches 105°C (221°F).

Remove the pan from the heat and leave to cool for 10 minutes, then whisk the foam on the top back into the jam and pour into warmed, sterilised jars (see page 13). Store in the refrigerator for up to 3 months.

Tips

- To make jam without pectin, grate ½ apple with the skin on. Add the grated apple to the saucepan along with the fruit, sugar and lemon juice, and follow the instructions as above.

- If you want to make strawberry jam, it's advisable to reduce the sugar quantity to 400 g (14 oz/1¾ cups) as strawberries have a lot of natural sweetness.

Candied Fruits

These are traditionally made at Christmastime, but we like to incorporate candied fruits into our bakes and desserts throughout the year. They add a wonderful sweet citrus note to our baking.

1 orange or pomelo, sliced into 5-mm (¼-in) rounds
1 lemon (ideally a variety with a thick peel), sliced into 5-mm (¼-in) rounds
725 g (1 lb 9½ oz/generous 3 cups) caster (superfine) sugar
500 g (2 cups) water
500 g (1 lb 2 oz) angelica stems (if you can find them), thinly sliced

Bring a large saucepan of water to the boil. Add your citrus fruit rounds to the pan of water and poach for just a few minutes.

Drain and refresh immediately in cold water (this will help the fruits to retain their colour and stop them cooking further).

Add 500 g (1 lb 2 oz/generous 2 cups) of the sugar and the measured fresh water to the empty pan and bring to the boil, then reduce to a simmer. Add your fruit slices to the simmering pot of syrup and cook slowly for about 10 minutes.

Remove from the heat and allow the fruits to cool entirely in the syrup.

Once completely cooled, add 75 g (⅓ cup) of the remaining sugar to the pan and bring the fruits and syrup to the boil again, then allow them to simmer for 1 minute. Remove from the heat and allow to cool.

Once cooled, repeat this step, adding another 75g (⅓ cup) of sugar.

Complete this step one final time, with the last 75 g (⅓ cup) of sugar.

When cool, transfer to an airtight container. Stored in their syrup, the candied fruits will keep in the refrigerator for up to 3 months. The leftover syrup can be used for glazing cakes.

5 hours
Makes 20-30 slices, or more if angelica is used

Preparation - 10 minutes
Cooking - 15 minutes

Cooling - 1 hour
+ 3 stages of 5 minutes cooking and 1 hour cooling

Cherry Compote

This can easily be made with frozen cherries and treated in the same way you would a jam. We like to keep this as a traditional compote and very chunky, but if you're using it in a cake or pudding you can lightly blitz it to make a purée. In the winter, we like to add some cloves and a cinnamon stick for a lovely spiced version of this compote.

500 g (1 lb 2 oz/2½ cups) fresh (or frozen) cherries, pitted
400 g (14 oz/1¾ cups) caster (superfine) sugar
50 g (3 tablespoons) lemon juice
1 vanilla pod
5 g (1½ teaspoons) pectin powder (or ½ apple, see note below)

Place a plate in the refrigerator or freezer to get cold.

Put all of the compote ingredients into a heavy-based saucepan set over a medium heat and stir together. Once the sugar has dissolved, bring to the boil, then reduce the heat and simmer until thickened, about 20 minutes.

To test whether your compote has reached setting point, take 1 teaspoon of the compote and place it on the cold plate. Allow to cool, then run your finger through it. If this leaves a clear run and the compote doesn't run back in on itself, the setting point has been reached.

Alternatively, once the compote is boiling, you can use a digital thermometer to measure the temperature. It will be ready when it reaches 105°C (221°F).

Remove the pan from the heat and leave to cool for 10 minutes, then remove the vanilla pod and pour into warmed, sterilised jars (see page 13). Store in the refrigerator for up to 3 months.

To make the compote without pectin

Grate ½ apple with the skin on. Add the grated apple to the saucepan along with the fruit, sugar and lemon juice, and follow the instructions as above.

40 minutes
Makes 2 x 330-g (11-oz) jars

Preparation – 10 minutes
Cooking – about 20 minutes
Cooling – 10 minutes

Spiced Apple Compote

This is another cheeseboard classic, but can also be used for the base of a frangipane tart or for adding to French toast, granola with yoghurt, the options are vast. This is the sort of thing everybody needs to have in their larder.

4 apples: 2 Bramley and 2 Granny
    Smith, peeled, cored and chopped
    into 5-mm (¼-in) dice
100 g (3½ oz/½ cup) sugar
    (any variety, but light brown
    is very good)
juice of 1 lemon
1 clove

Put all of the compote ingredients into a heavy-based saucepan set over the lowest heat and stir together. Cover with the lid and cook slowly for 30 minutes until thickened. Check and stir occasionally to make sure it's not sticking to the bottom of the pan.

Remove from the heat and allow to cool completely. Remove the clove.

It can be kept as a more chunky apple compote or whizzed in a food processor to make it completely smooth.

Store in an airtight container or in sterilised jars (see page 13) in the refrigerator for up to 1 month.

Apple and Mango Chutney

Chutneys are such a lovely thing to have in your store cupboard. With just a few simple ingredients you can make the most wonderful meal. Take some freshly baked sourdough, a selection of cheeses and charcuterie and a generous helping of this chutney and you've got the most sensational take on a Ploughman's, just bursting with flavour.

20 ml (1½ tablespoons) rapeseed (canola) oil
500 g (1 lb 2 oz) cooking apples, peeled, cored and cut into chunky dice
1 mango, peeled and flesh cut away from stone, cut into chunky dice
50 g (2 oz) preserved ginger, minced
125 g (4 oz/⅔ cup) soft dark brown sugar
125 g (½ cup) apple cider vinegar
125 g (½ cup) water
¾ teaspoon fine sea salt
½ teaspoon nigella (black onion) seeds
½ teaspoon ground cumin
½ teaspoon ground cardamom
½ teaspoon ground cloves
½ teaspoon ground cinnamon
1 bay leaf

Heat the oil in a large saucepan over a medium heat. Add the apple and mango and cook until soft, about 5 minutes.

Add the remaining ingredients to the pan and cook slowly, stirring occasionally, until the liquid has almost evaporated, about 50 minutes. Increase the heat slightly and continue to stir for about 5 more minutes until the mixture is sticky.

Remove from the heat and leave to cool, then transfer the chutney to sterilised jars (see page 13) and seal securely with lids.

Store in the refrigerator for up to 1 month.

Bread and Butter Pickles

Perfect with a ham sandwich or most cured meats, these quick pickles are very versatile and can be eaten for breakfast, lunch and dinner.

1 kg (2 lb 4 oz) small cucumbers (the Lebanese variety are great), sliced into 1-cm (½-in) thick rounds
1 medium onion, cut into thick slices
60 g (2 oz/½ cup) flaked sea salt
500 g (2 cups) apple cider vinegar
400 g (14 oz/1⅔ cups) caster (superfine) sugar
½ teaspoon ground turmeric
1 tablespoon cumin seeds
1 tablespoon yellow or brown mustard seeds
6 whole peppercorns
few sprigs of fresh dill (optional)

Add the cucumbers, onions and salt to a mixing bowl and toss together, ensuring the salt gets well worked through the onions and cucumber. Transfer the mixture to a sieve (fine-mesh strainer) and set it over the mixing bowl. Place in the refrigerator for 1–2 hours – this process will encourage all of the excess water to drain out of the cucumbers, giving a really crunchy pickle.

Add the vinegar, sugar and spices to a saucepan set over a medium heat and bring to the boil, then reduce the heat and simmer for 4–5 minutes.

Remove from the heat and allow to cool slightly.

Pack the drained cucumbers and onions into two large glass jars (about 1 kg/4 cups capacity each) pressing them down well. If using, press the sprigs of fresh dill into the jar at this point too. Dill gives a great flavour to pickles.

Pour over the cooled vinegar mixture and seal the jar. Store in the refrigerator. Try to leave the pickles for at least a day to infuse before tucking in. They should keep for up to 2 weeks stored in the refrigerator.

1 hour 20 minutes
(plus at least 1 day resting)
Makes 2 x 1-kg (4-cup) jars

Preparation - 15 minutes
Chilling - 1-2 hours
Cooking - 5-6 minutes
Resting - at least 1 day

Red Onion Marmalade

This is really classic and a staple for your pantry. Served with cheese, terrine or freshly toasted sourdough bread, it makes a lovely addition.

40 ml (2½ tablespoons) rapeseed (canola) oil
1 kg (2 lb 4 oz) red onions, sliced
250 g (9 oz/1⅓ cups) dark brown sugar
250 ml (1 cup) red wine vinegar
250 ml (1 cup) water
15 g (2¼ teaspoons) fine salt
10 sprigs of fresh thyme, leaves picked
1 bay leaf

Heat the oil in a large saucepan over a medium heat. Add the onions and cook until soft but not coloured, about 15 minutes.

Add the remaining ingredients to the pan and cook slowly until the liquid has almost evaporated, about 50 minutes. Increase the heat slightly and continue to stir until the mixture is sticky.

Remove from the heat and leave to cool, then transfer the marmalade to sterilised jars (see page 13) and seal securely with lids.

Store in the refrigerator for up to 1 month.

2 hours 15 minutes
Makes 3 x 330-g (11-oz) jars

Preparation – 10 minutes
Cooking – about 1 hour
Cooling – 1 hour

Bread Ahead Mincemeat

You can start mincemeat up to three months in advance, as it will keep happily and improves a little with age. I like to play with the spices each year to make it unique. One year, I put in a little extra ground clove, which was spectacular.

125 g (4 oz) cooking apples, peeled, cored and finely diced
125 g (4 oz/1 cup) sultanas (golden raisins)
125 g (4 oz/generous ¾ cup) currants
125 g (4 oz/1 cup) raisins
500 g (1 lb 2 oz/4½ cups) shredded suet (or grated frozen vegetable shortening)
125 g (4 oz/⅔ cup) soft dark brown sugar
35 g (1¼ oz/⅓ cup) nibbed or flaked (slivered) almonds
1½ teaspoons mixed spice
½ teaspoon ground cinnamon
½ teaspoon grated nutmeg
zest and juice of 1 lemon
zest and juice of 1 orange
60 ml (4 tablespoons) brandy (optional)
1 tablespoon dark rum (optional)

Day 1

Put all of the ingredients, apart from the brandy and rum, if using, into a very large mixing bowl and mix together. Cover and leave overnight in a cool place (but not the refrigerator).

Day 2

Preheat the oven to 120°C (100°C fan/gas ¼). Line a large deep roasting tray (pan) with baking paper.

Place all the mincemeat mixture into the prepared tray and bake for 1 hour, stirring every 20 minutes.

Remove from the oven and leave to cool for about 30 minutes.

Stir in the brandy and rum, if using, and pack into sterilised jars (see page 13). Store in a cool, dark place for up to 3 months.

2 days
Makes enough to fill
12 mince pies

Day 1
Preparation - 10 minutes
Resting - overnight

Stage 2
Baking - 1 hour
Finishing - 45 minutes

Index

Acknowledgements

Thanks are due to

Our suppliers: Marriage's Millers, whose dedication to their craft is evident in everything they do. They are an indispensable part of Bread Ahead. Campbell, who produces such fine quality baking supplies – a true craftsman. AEG, for their generous support in making our bakery school classrooms first rate. PG Tips, because we couldn't live without all those brews during a long shift in the bakery.

The Bread Ahead team: The bakery school teachers and assistants who work so hard to make the Bread Ahead bakery school what it is. We know from the feedback we receive every week from home bakers who pass through the schools just how valued our school team really are. Chris Malec, who has been instrumental in shaping Bread Ahead as we know it today (he also shapes a pretty mean sourdough these days). And Nadia Ismail, who is both our marketing ninja and a fine baker.

The book team: Kajal and Emily, our editors, who gave such thoughtful feedback and encouragement and have helped to create a truly memorable book. Designers Evi, Susan and Wilson, for outstanding work. Photographer Matt and the shoot team Kitty, Jen, Hannah, Valeria and Jo have honestly created something visually beautiful – we are deeply grateful for your hard work and input. And Iona Kong, who on many occasions brought our bakes to life with beautiful photography – it's been a pleasure working with you.

Our neighbours at Borough Market, Ginger Pig and Turnips, who share our ethos for exceptional quality and seasonal produce – we thoroughly enjoy sitting alongside you.

We also want to thank our landlords, Borough Market, Cadogan, Wembley Park and Quintain Living, for the communities they have created across London and for their continuous support of the Bread Ahead vision and journey.

Finally, we want to thank the Bread Ahead fans, supporters and food lovers: @triplets_in_my_kitchen, for bringing so much fun to home baking.

KS from @ks_ate_here, for your constant enthusiasm and genuine love of all things food.

Gezza – a long-standing fan of Bread Ahead. We admire your enthusiasm and home baking skills.

Slow Food – for being an example of how food should be treated and respected, thank you for the support over many years.

And to every single person who tuned into an IG live baking tutorial or e-learning workshop, or shared a photo of their home bakes and have made this baking community one that we're so proud to be a part of.

Gas	°F	°C	°C Fan
¼	225	110	90
½	250	120	100
1	275	130/140	110/120
2	300	150	130
3	325	160	140
4	350	170/180	150/160
5	375	190	170
6	400	200/210	180/190
7	425	220	200
8	450	230	210
9	475	240/250	220/230
10	500	240	240

This book is dedicated to
my Mum, my wife Erika
& our son Magnus Francis.

Published in 2021 by Hardie Grant Books,
an imprint of Hardie Grant Publishing

Hardie Grant Books (London)
5th & 6th Floors
52–54 Southwark Street
London SE1 1UN

Hardie Grant Books (Melbourne)
Building 1, 658 Church Street
Richmond, Victoria 3121

hardiegrantbooks.com

British Library Cataloguing-in-Publication Data. A catalogue
record for this book is available from the British Library.

Bread Ahead: The Expert Home Baker
ISBN: 9-781-78488-446-8

10 9 8 7 6 5 4 3 2 1

Publisher: Kajal Mistry
Project Editor: Emily Preece-Morrison
Design and Illustrations: Evi-O. Studio | Susan Le
Photographer: Matt Russell
Food Stylist: Kitty Coles
Prop Stylist: Jennifer Kay
Photography Assistant: Hannah Lemon
Food Assistants: Valeria Russo and Joanna Jackson
Proofreader: Vicky Orchard
Indexer: Vanessa Bird
Production Controller: Nikolaus Ginelli

Colour reproduction by p2d
Printed and bound in China by Leo Paper Products Ltd.

MIX
Paper from
responsible sources
FSC™ C020056
FSC
www.fsc.org